never broken

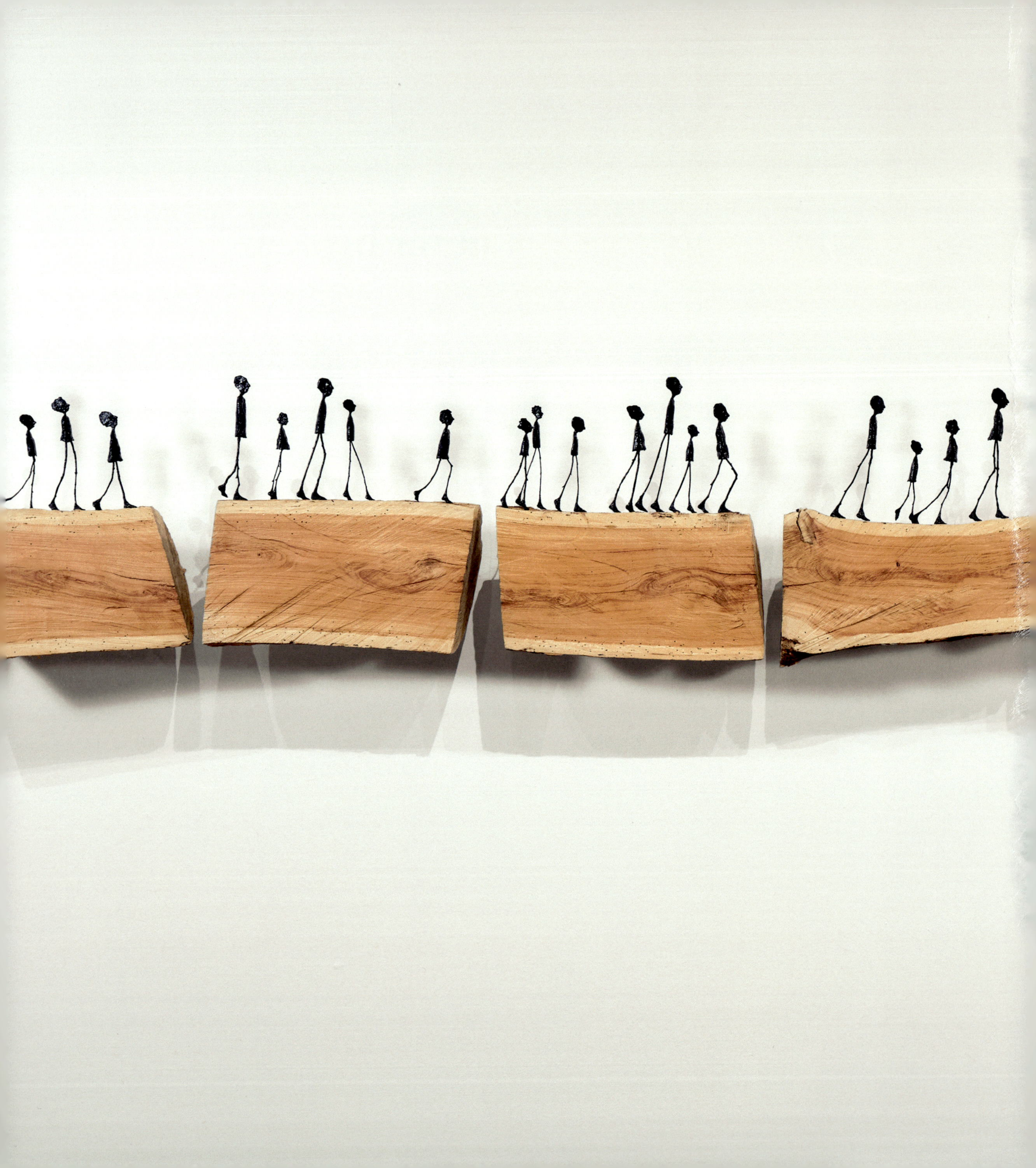

never broken

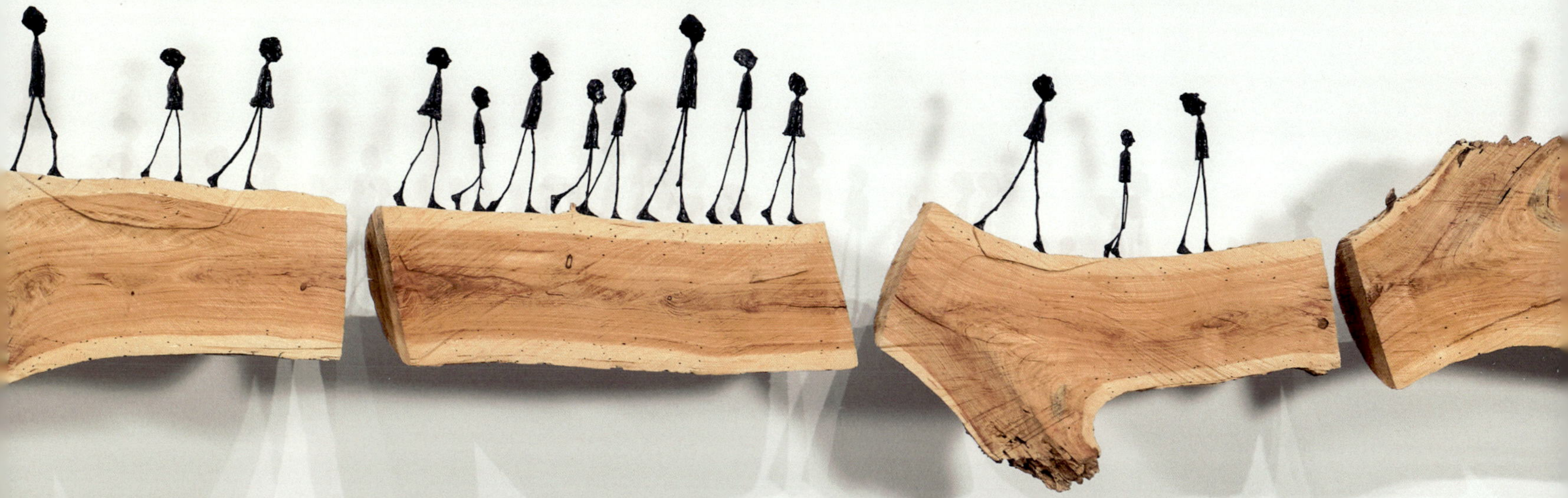

Visualizing Lenape Histories

*Edited by Joe Baker
and Laura Turner Igoe*

JAMES A. MICHENER ART MUSEUM
UNIVERSITY OF PENNSYLVANIA PRESS

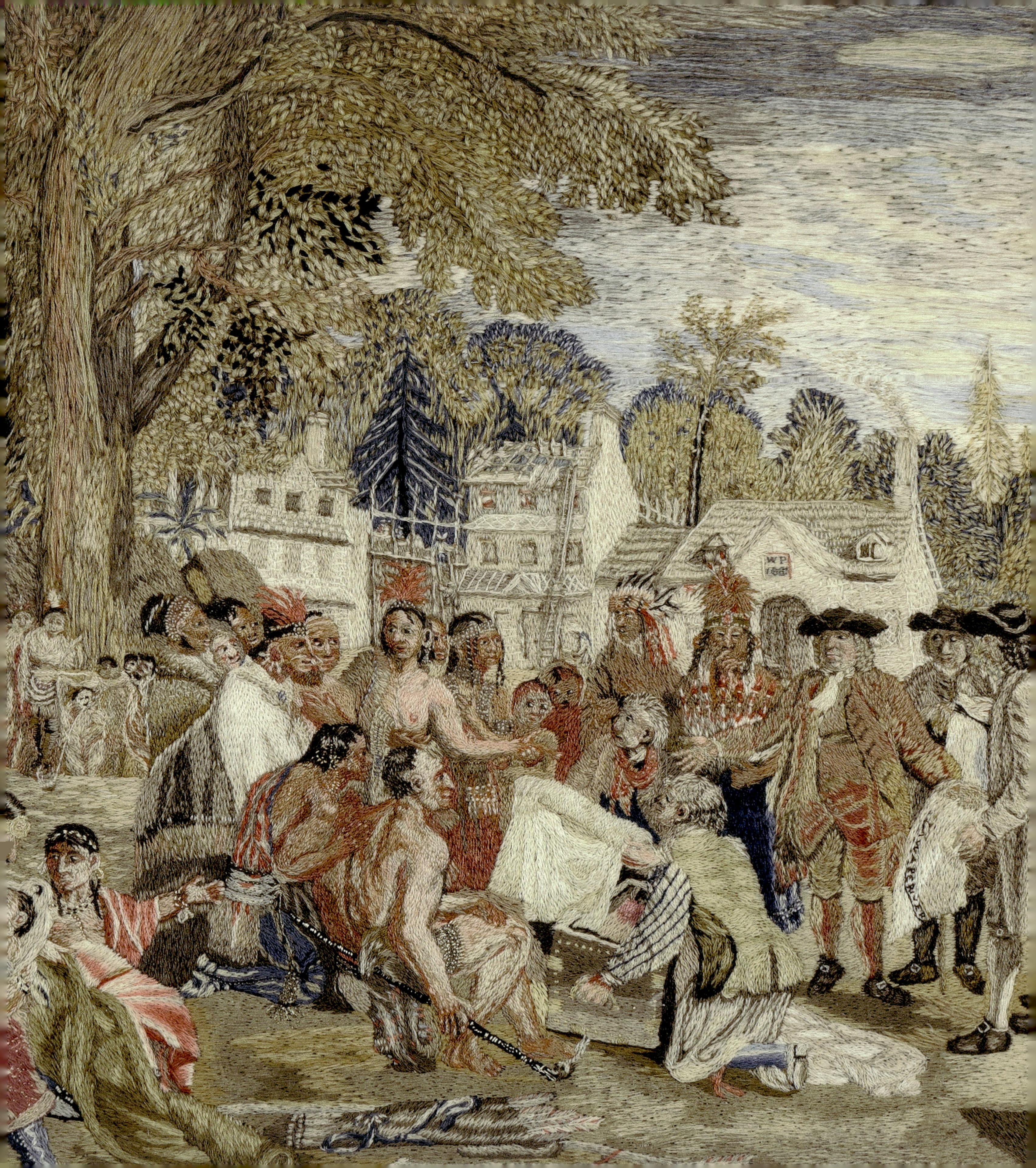

Contents

Detail of plate 9

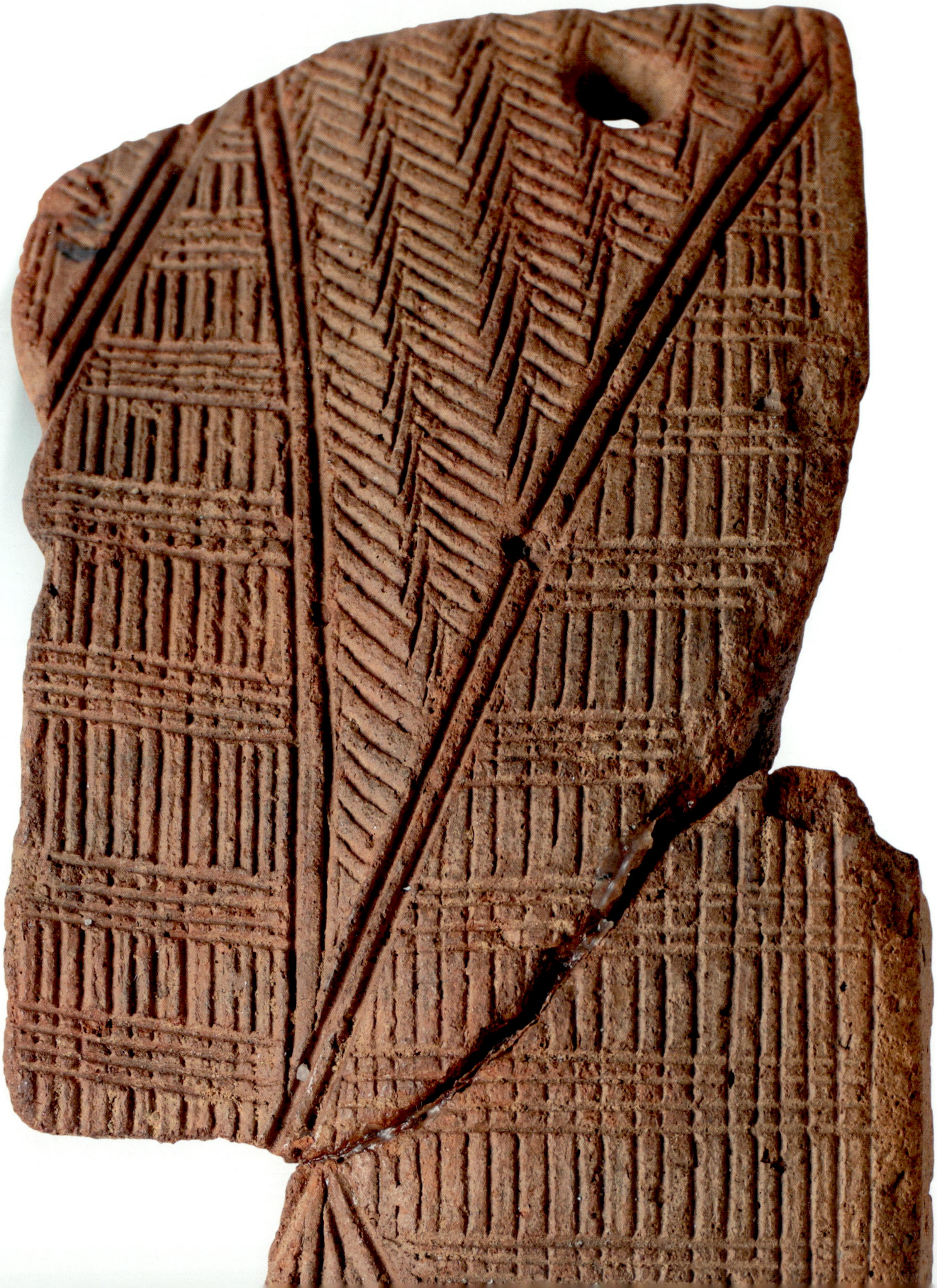

Foreword and Acknowledgments

ON MAY 2, 2023, IN GREAT ANTICIPATION OF THE PLANNED *Never Broken* exhibition, Lenape Center co-founder and co-director Curtis Zunigha shared the history of the Lenape homeland with the Michener Art Museum staff and board members. You could have heard a pin drop as he spoke, and his words made us think about our perceptions of history.

The exhibition *Never Broken: Visualizing Lenape Histories* provides a context for understanding and appreciating how art can explore, challenge, and foster learning about that history. I am thrilled that the Michener Art Museum was able to organize this important exhibition with the Lenape Center and bring it to Bucks County. I am hopeful that it will engage people in a deeper reflection on the heritage of this beautiful land.

I would like to thank co-curators Laura Turner Igoe and Joe Baker and the exhibition lenders, including the Philadelphia Museum of Art, Brooklyn Museum, Winterthur Museum, New Jersey State Museum, Mercer Museum, and Thomas Cleary. I extend our gratitude to the participating artists—Joe Baker, Ahchipaptunhe (David L. Haff), Holly Wilson, and Nathan Young—whose thought-provoking work will help visitors to develop their own understanding and appreciation of history. Thank you to Joel Whitney for his thoughtful contributions to this catalogue, and the folks at Brilliant Graphics and Marquand Books, including Bob Tursack, Dustin Tursack, Gina Broze, Adrian Lucia, Kestrel Rundle, Tom Eykemans, and Bruno George, for their production of a beautiful book.

The exhibition is one in a series of American art exhibitions created through a multi-year, multi-institutional partnership formed by the Philadelphia Museum of Art as part of the Art Bridges Cohort Program. Major support for this exhibition and catalogue was provided by the Henry Luce Foundation with additional support from the Michener Art Museum's Corporate Business Partners, Eiseman Construction, Inc., and the Dolfinger-McMahon Foundation. We are grateful for their support.

Finally, I wish also to thank my Michener colleagues for their support and commitment to this exhibition and catalogue.

Dr. Vail P. Garvin
Executive Director, James A. Michener Art Museum

Detail of plate 4

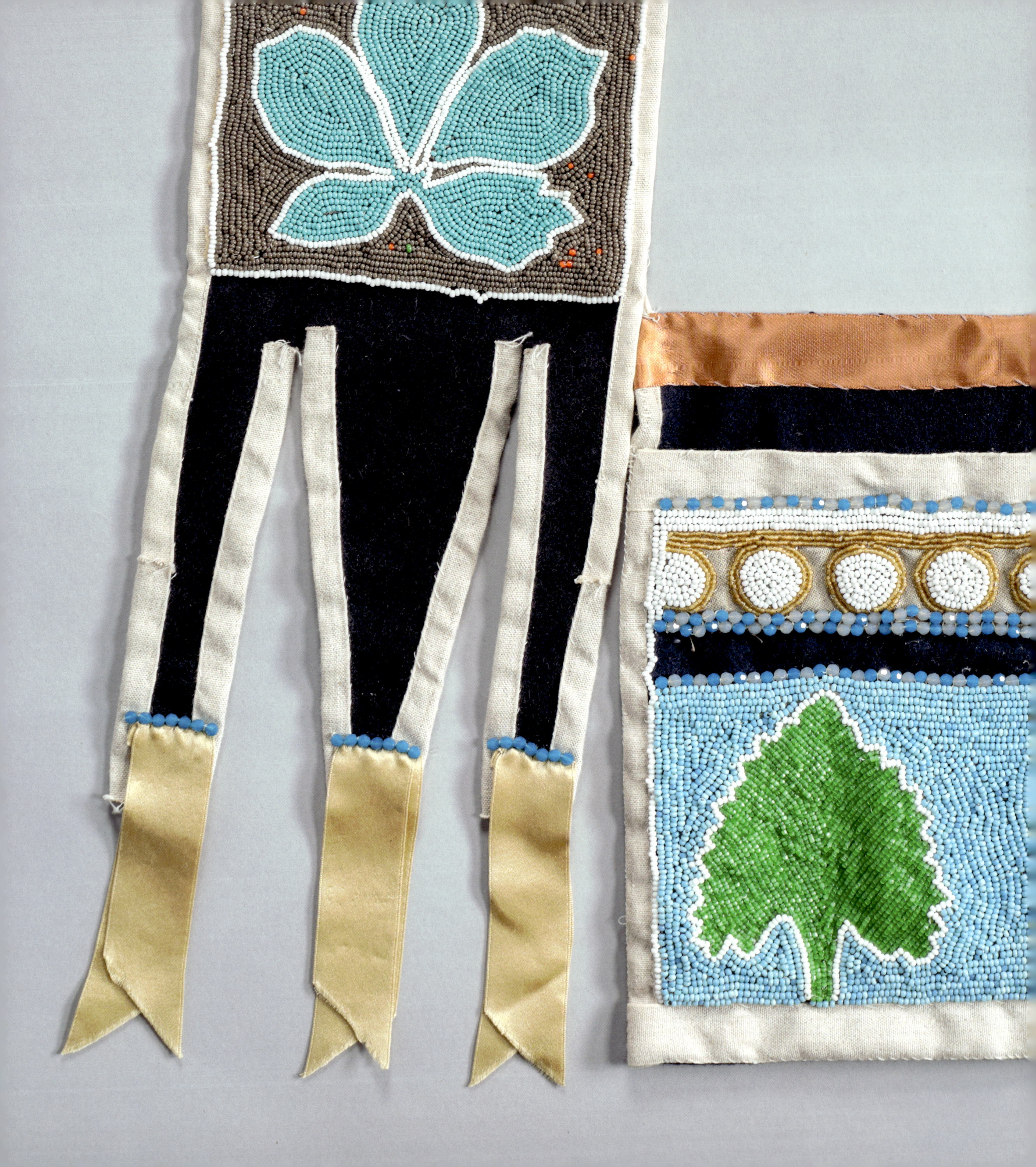

Introduction

Joe Baker and Laura Turner Igoe

Detail of plate 30

THIS VOLUME, PUBLISHED IN CONJUNCTION WITH THE exhibition *Never Broken: Visualizing Lenape Histories*, considers the power of art to construct and dismantle inaccurate Indigenous histories. In the exhibition, on view at the James A. Michener Art Museum from September 9, 2023, to January 14, 2024, contemporary art by Ahchipaptunhe (Delaware Tribe of Indians and Cherokee), Joe Baker (Delaware Tribe of Indians), Holly Wilson (Delaware Nation and Cherokee), and Nathan Young (Delaware Tribe of Indians, Pawnee, and Kiowa) is displayed in dialogue with historic Lenape ceramics, beadwork, and other cultural objects as well as with re-creations, by European American artists, of Benjamin West's painting *Penn's Treaty with the Indians*. The Native American artworks in this exhibition express personal and tribal identity and address the Lenape's violent displacement from Lenapehoking, the Lenape homeland that encompasses the region where the Michener Art Museum currently stands.

Never Broken: Visualizing Lenape Histories is the first exhibition of Native American art organized by the Michener Art Museum and, as Joe Baker notes in his essay, the first exhibition of contemporary Lenape artists in Pennsylvania who can trace their families back to the time of the Walking Purchase and William Penn. The Michener, located in Doylestown, Pennsylvania, is very close to the route that three representatives of Pennsylvania's proprietary government ran over a day and a half in the infamous Walking Purchase land swindle of 1737 in order to claim 1.2 million acres of land northeast of Doylestown. For many years, the Lenape were resistant to relinquishing the prime hunting grounds in the area now known as Bucks County, Pennsylvania, to William Penn and his agents, threatening violence to protect this remaining stronghold.[1] The Walking Purchase wrested this significant land away from the Lenape. *Never Broken* allows the Michener and its visitors to contend with this history that occurred so close to its walls and to share a Lenape perspective on these past events through historic and contemporary art.

The Michener Art Museum is honored to partner with Joe Baker and the Lenape Center for this exhibition and catalogue. Founded in 2009, Lenape Center, a nonprofit art and culture organization, has been working to push back against the erasure of Lenape people, their stories, and their histories through innovative exhibitions and programs in the ancestral homeland. By challenging established pathways that have been built without recognition of the original people, Lenape Center secures a future of cultural vibrancy for the coming generations.

The objects and art displayed in *Never Broken* celebrate the legacy and evolution of Lenape visual expression and cross-cultural exchange. Inscribed Lenape ceramics from the Middle and Late Woodland periods (200–1600 CE) (Plates 1–4) and stamped splint wood baskets (Plates 5–6) with abstract floral and leaf motifs illuminate the Lenape's ancestral and spiritual connection to this land prior to the arrival of European colonists, presenting Turtle Island (North America) as a place of vibrant cultural exchange. A series of large-scale abstract paintings by Ahchipaptunhe (Plates 32–35), commissioned for the exhibition, responds to the geometric forms and shapes inscribed on these vessels. Nineteenth-century bandolier bags (Plates 21–22) and a pair of moccasins (Plate 23), made by Lenape women and worn by Lenape men to complement ceremonial outfits, utilize glass beads imported from Venice, trade cloth, and printed cotton, demonstrating the significance of cross-cultural exchange to Lenape creative expression. After learning that white collectors had removed many historic bandolier bags from his Delaware Tribe community, Joe Baker taught himself how to make these beaded bags (Plates 28–30), combining traditional Lenape iconography with more personal symbols and motifs. According to Baker, "my hope was to bring this art form back to our people in our community."[2] Paintings by Baker (Plates 24–27) and Holly Wilson's sculpture *Bloodline* (Plate 31) explore the artists' lineage and tribal identity. Finally, *Alëmi pëmëske* (*He begins to walk*) (Plate 37), a video and sound piece by Nathan Young, reverses, and therefore visually unmakes, the route of the Walking Purchase, as Young and fellow artist Yatika Fields walk on eighteen miles of modern roads from Ottsville, Pennsylvania, where Solomon Jennings, one of the three "walkers," dropped out due to exhaustion, to Wrightstown Friends Meeting, where the race began.

Altogether, these historic and contemporary artworks provide a counternarrative to one perpetuated by the arguably best-known painting of Native and Anglo-American negotiations: *Penn's Treaty with the Indians* by Benjamin West (Fig. 1). In the first essay of this volume, Laura Turner Igoe critically interrogates the plethora of prints, paintings, and decorative arts that incorporate imagery from West's iconic painting. West's composition depicted a treaty of peace between the Pennsylvania province's founder William Penn and the Lenape that was praised by Anglo-Americans as "never broken." This scene went viral in a pre-internet age, appearing on textiles, fine porcelain, and other printed material in the late eighteenth and nineteenth centuries. Bucks County painter Edward Hicks (1780–1849) appropriated West's composition for his own paintings of *Penn's Treaty* (Plates 15–17) and incorporated the scene into his well-known *Peaceable Kingdom* series (Plate 18). Igoe argues that this viral imagery, which proliferated over a century after the depicted event, attempted to rewrite the fraught history of Native and Anglo-American conflict with a myth of peaceful coexistence and succession.

Joel Whitney's essay provides an overview of the culture of the Lenape and their forced removal. Despite the Lenape's hospitality to European colonists and their reputation as shrewd negotiators, their treaties and agreements were continually violated, including the 1778 Treaty of Fort Pitt, which proposed an Indigenous state under the Lenape with representation in Congress. The murder of the treaty's Lenape signatory, Koquethagechton (1730–1778), known as Chief White Eyes, that same year, rescinded this astounding offer. Over the following century, the Lenape were violently forced out of Pennsylvania and the northeast, settling in Oklahoma, Wisconsin, and Ontario.

Finally, Joe Baker brings together the words of artists Ahchipaptunhe, Holly Wilson, and Nathan Young, as well as Jim Rementer, the Delaware Tribe's language keeper, in order to highlight how Lenape artists today tell their own stories rooted in memory, ancestry, oral history, and connection to Lenapehoking. Baker, along with the listed artists, challenges the myth making and propaganda of the American experience through the sharing of his own family history.

Through a focus on Lenape art and culture and a critical examination of historical visualizations of Native and European American relationships, *Never Broken* demonstrates the ways in which art can create, challenge, and rewrite history.

The artworks featured in the exhibition and the catalogue assert that the Lenape are still here and have their own powerful stories to tell in the face of historical erasure and marginalization.

Notes

1 Jean R. Soderland, *Lenape Country: Delaware Valley Society Before William Penn* (Philadelphia: University of Pennsylvania Press, 2015), 149.

2 Benjamin Korman, "Committing to the Beauty of Lenape Art," *Perspectives*, Metropolitan Museum of Art, November 23, 2021, https://www.metmuseum.org/perspectives/articles/2021/11/joe-baker-lenape-bandolier-bag.

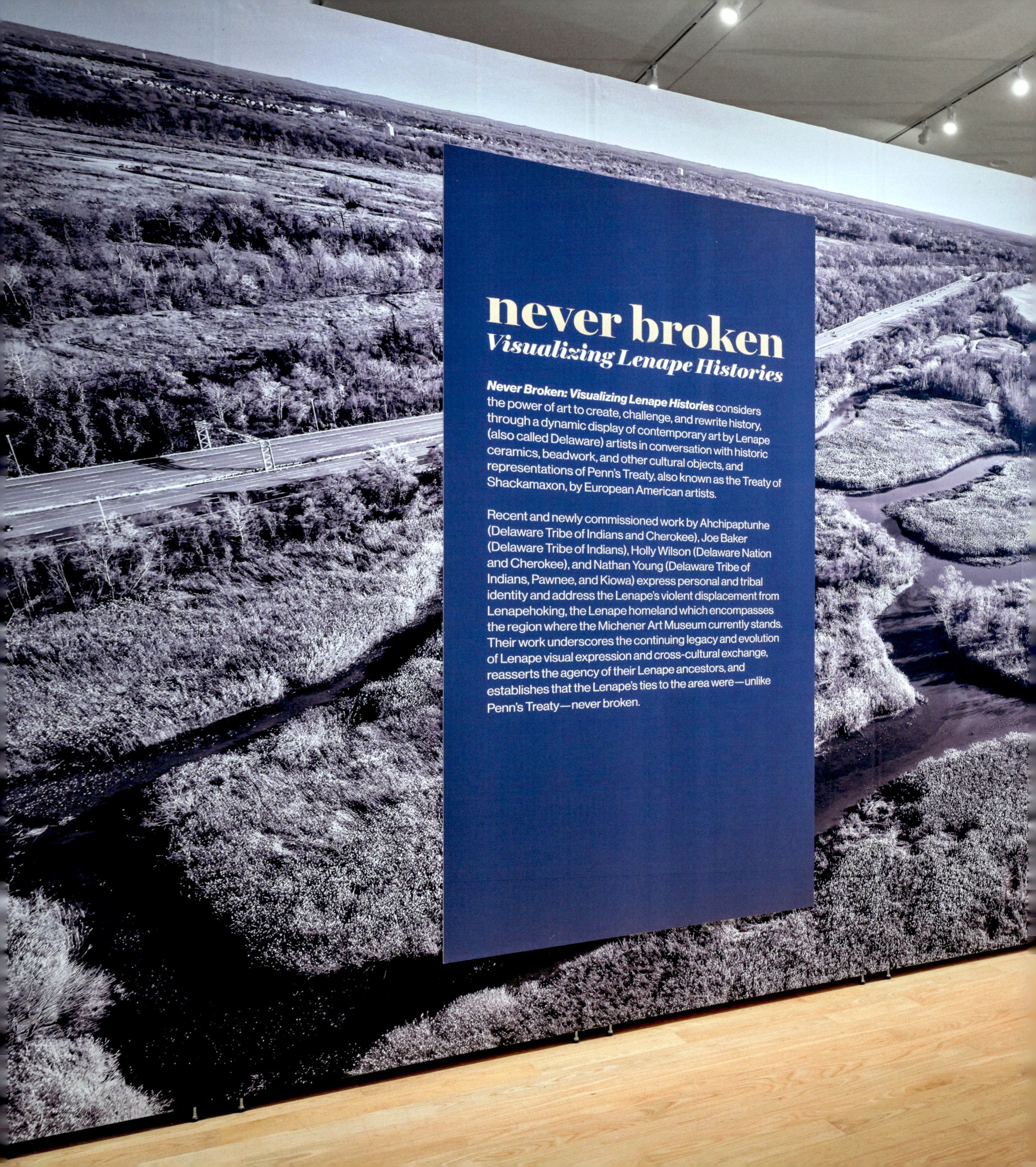
never broken
Visualizing Lenape Histories
Never Broken: Visualizing Lenape Histories considers the power of art to create, challenge, and rewrite history, through a dynamic display of contemporary art by Lenape (also called Delaware) artists in conversation with historic ceramics, beadwork, and other cultural objects, and representations of Penn's Treaty, also known as the Treaty of Shackamaxon, by European American artists.
Recent and newly commissioned work by Ahchipaptunhe (Delaware Tribe of Indians and Cherokee), Joe Baker (Delaware Tribe of Indians), Holly Wilson (Delaware Nation and Cherokee), and Nathan Young (Delaware Tribe of Indians, Pawnee, and Kiowa) express personal and tribal identity and address the Lenape's violent displacement from Lenapehoking, the Lenape homeland which encompasses the region where the Michener Art Museum currently stands. Their work underscores the continuing legacy and evolution of Lenape visual expression and cross-cultural exchange, reasserts the agency of their Lenape ancestors, and establishes that the Lenape's ties to the area were—unlike Penn's Treaty—never broken.

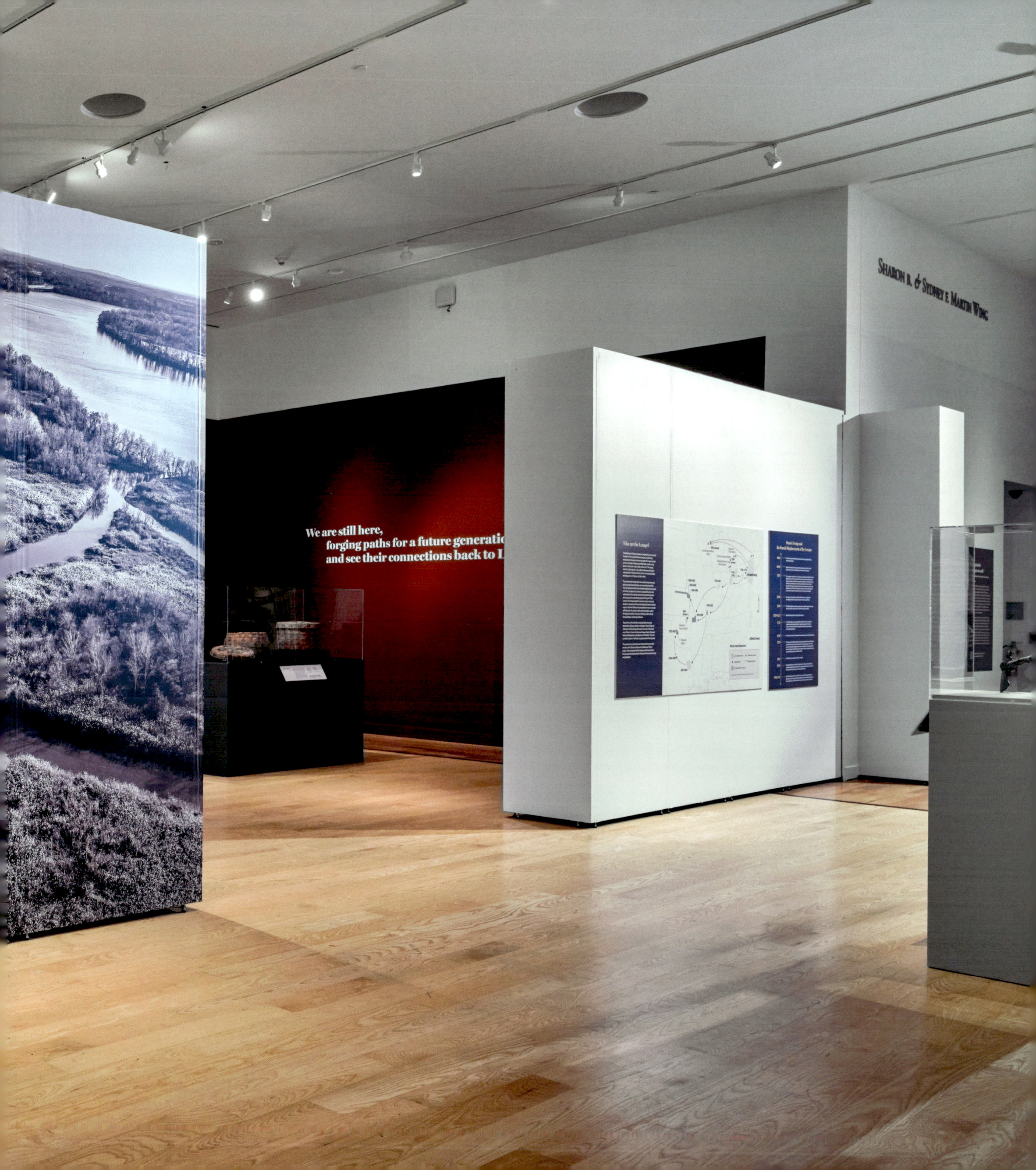
Sharon B. & Sydney F. Martin Wing
We are still here,
forging paths for a future generatio
and see their connections back to L

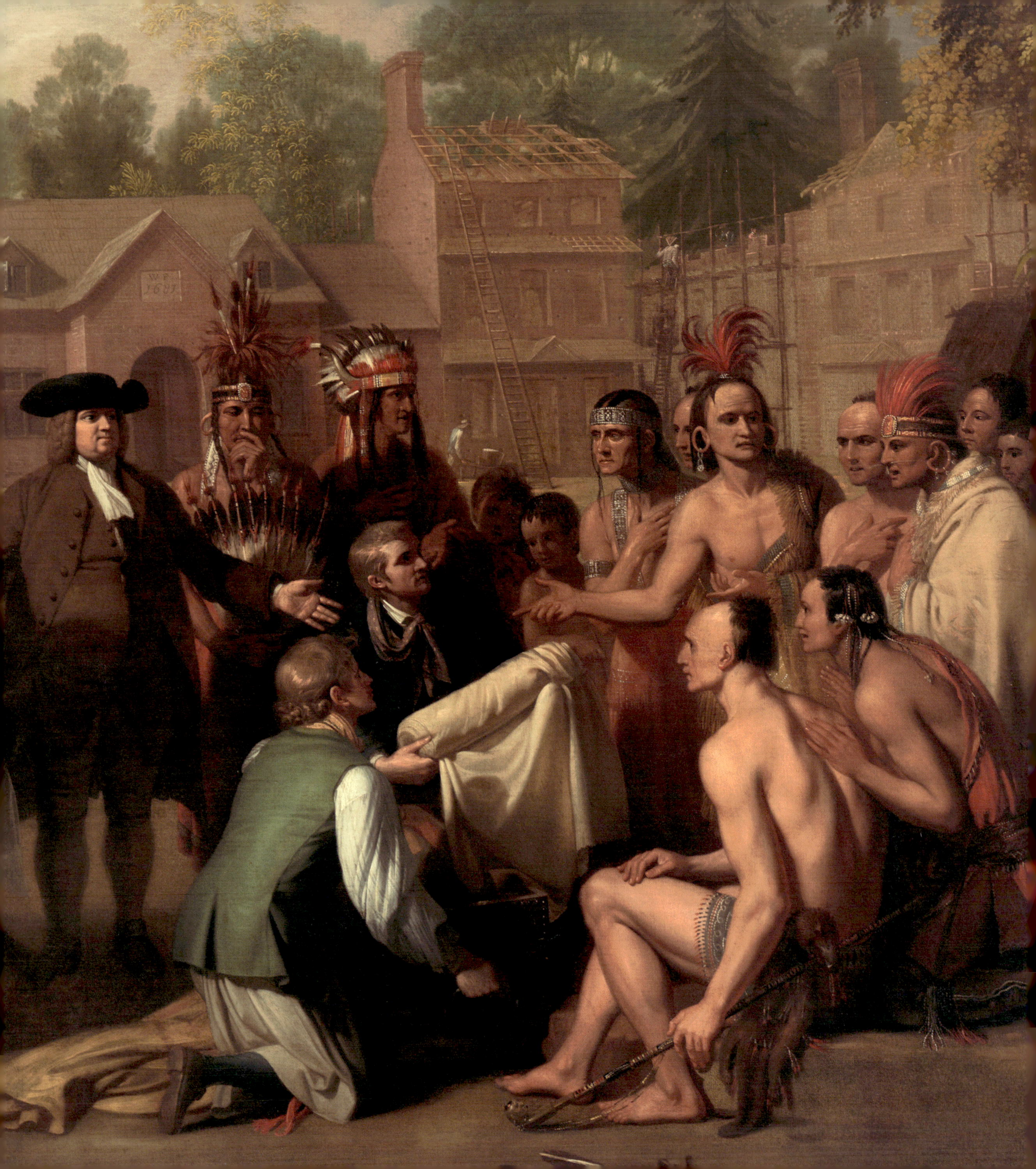
W P

Penn's Treaty with the Indians

Myth-Making across Media

Laura Turner Igoe

Detail of figure 1

IN 1772, *PENN'S TREATY WITH THE INDIANS* (FIG. 1) BY THE American-born artist Benjamin West (1738–1820) belatedly established a visual record for an event with a murky history and limited documentation that had occurred over a century prior. In West's composition, a group of Quakers in dark tricornered hats meets with a group of Lenape, the Indigenous people who resided in Lenapehoking, or the Lenape homeland, which encompassed land from present-day Delaware to Connecticut. In the center of the painting, two merchants present a bolt of cloth to several Lenape, who animatedly discuss its merits. William Penn (1644–1718), the founder of the province of Pennsylvania, stands left of center with his arms outspread, gesturing to an unrolled piece of parchment with his right hand and the cloth with his left. A bow and a clutch of arrows lie discarded in the foreground of the painting, and the central seated Lenape figure holds a peace pipe in his hand, emphasizing the diplomatic nature of the meeting. Two figural groupings bookend the central scene in the foreground, forming a triptych-like composition. To the left, two merchants lounge on crates of their merchandise in front of a harbor populated with several ships. In the right foreground, a Lenape woman nurses her child, who is wrapped to a cradleboard, while an older child next to her gestures to the central exchange. A series of brick buildings under construction rises in the background.

Shortly after it was exhibited at the Royal Academy in London in 1772, West's painting was copied by John Hall (1739–1797), who produced an engraving (Plate 8) of it for the publisher John Boydell (1719–1804) that was subsequently disseminated throughout the Atlantic World. This image essentially went viral in a pre-internet age, appearing on textiles, fine china, and other printed material that could be purchased and consumed at a relatively low price. As a result, *Penn's Treaty* appeared in a variety of unusual places, from an illustrated book of American costumes published in Milan (Plate 13) to a painting on metal by an unidentified artist (Plate 14). The Bucks County, Pennsylvania, painter Edward Hicks (1780–1849) copied the scene multiple times (Plates 14–17) and incorporated it into his many *Peaceable Kingdom* paintings (Plate 18). Only a few decades after the publication of the *Penn's Treaty* engraving, the elm tree under which it was believed the treaty occurred fell down in a storm.

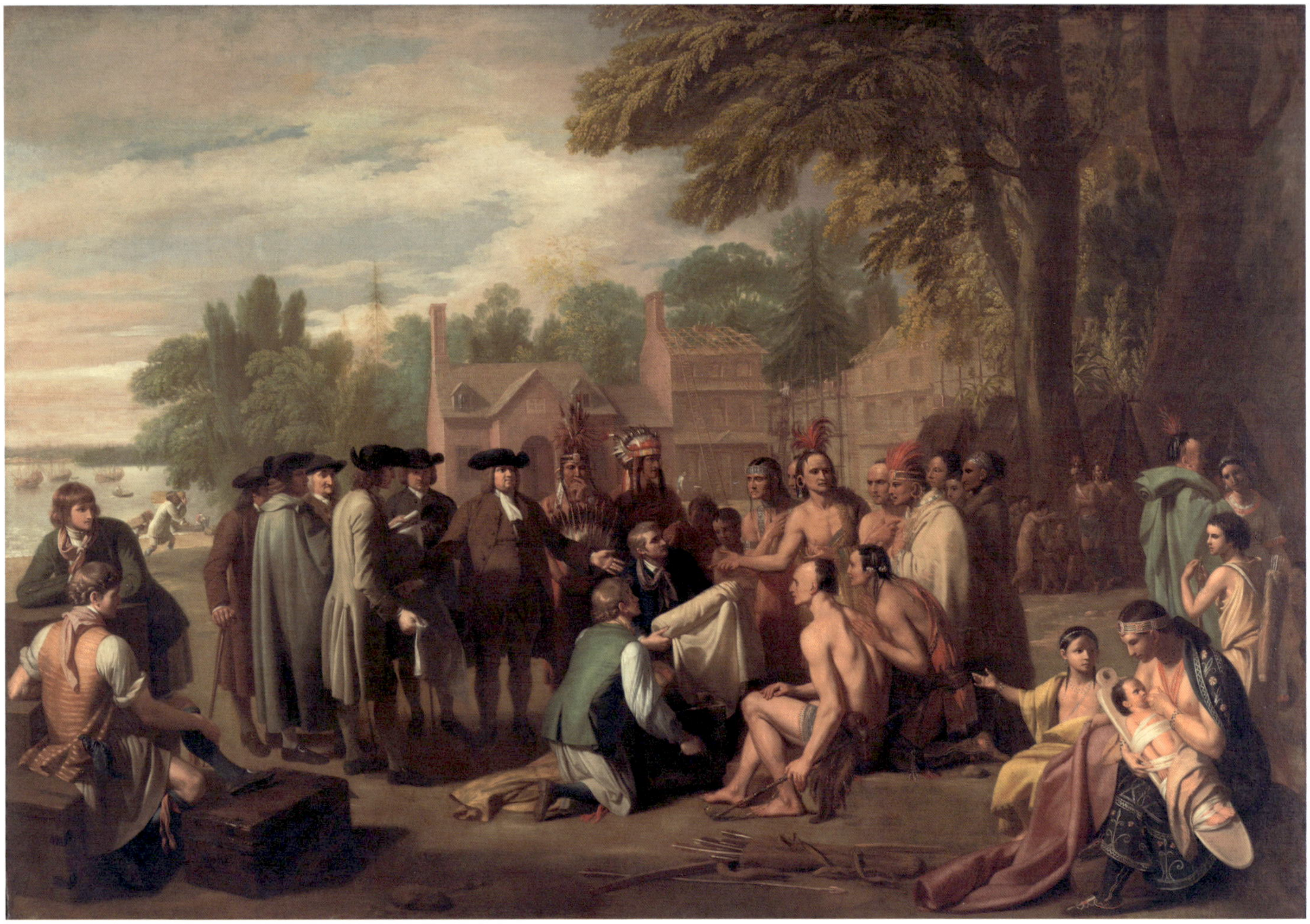

FIG. 1 Benjamin West, *Penn's Treaty with the Indians*, 1771–1772. Oil on canvas, 75½ × 107¾ inches. Courtesy of the Pennsylvania Academy of the Fine Arts, Philadelphia. Gift of Mrs. Sarah Harrison (The Joseph Harrison, Jr. Collection), 1878.1.10

After its fall, enterprising antiquarians, collectors, and carvers gathered the elm's wood to preserve as fragments or convert into various artifacts or relics (Plate 20), facilitating a material interaction with this mythic past event on an intimate level.

These tangible and obtainable items visually and materially associated with Penn's Treaty, while inarguably created to commemorate the memory of William Penn and reinforce ideological values of the young United States, were also attempts to rewrite the fraught history of Native and Anglo-American conflict with a myth of peaceful coexistence and fair exchange. Treaty Elm relics and consumable goods branded with West's image were so potent that they overwrote decades of deceitful and violent displacement of the Lenape people by Anglo-Americans. These images and objects also offered to their European American consumers a palatable creation myth for the United States, reassuring Quakers and other colonists that "their" Pennsylvania land was fairly acquired from, and willingly ceded by, the Lenape. A couple of later *Penn's Treaty* paintings by Edward Hicks (Fig. 2) further underscored this belief through the artist's addition of text stating that Penn's agreement with the Lenape was "made without an Oath and never broken. The foundation of Religious and Civil Liberty in the U.S. of America." *Penn's Treaty* and its many copies and appropriations demonstrate the power of visual arts and material culture to construct powerful historical narratives that still reverberate across our media landscape

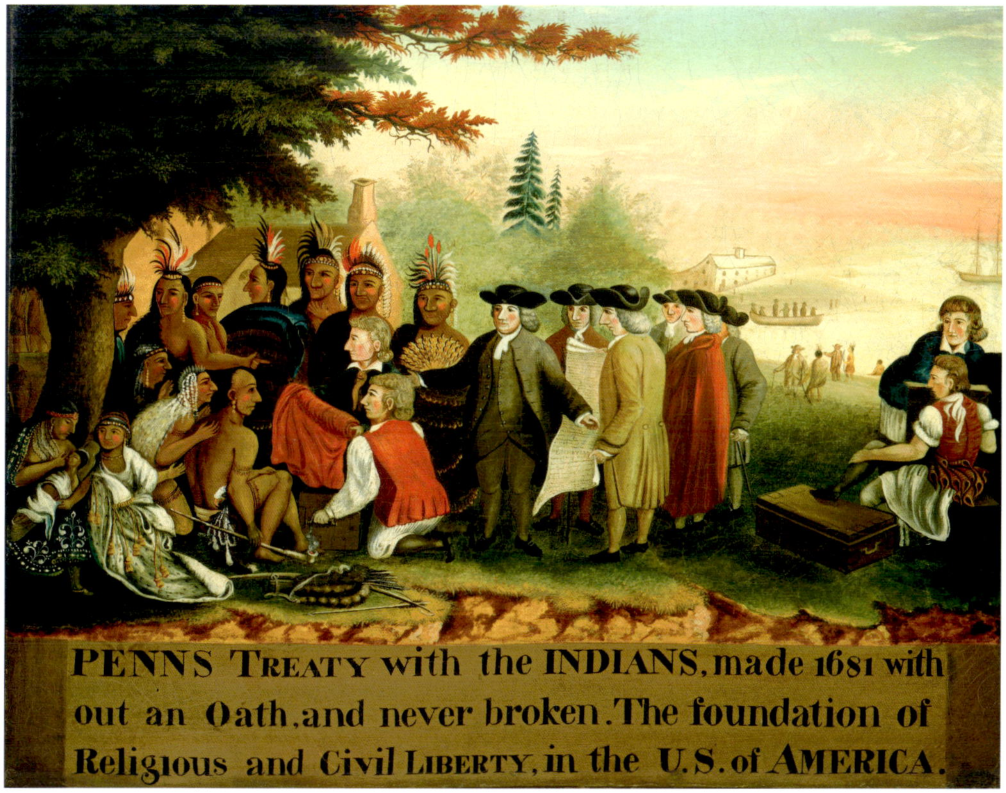

FIG. 2 Edward Hicks, *Penn's Treaty with the Indians*, ca. 1840–1844. Oil on canvas, $24\frac{5}{16} \times 30\frac{1}{8}$ inches. Gift of Edgar William and Bernice Chrysler Garbisch. Courtesy National Gallery of Art, Washington

today, as West's painting appears in modern-day textbooks and advertisements.

Constructing a Fictional Past

West painted *Penn's Treaty* at a time of great social, political, and economic instability in the British colonies of North America. Several scholars have highlighted West's anachronisms, distortions, and imperial iconography in the iconic painting, demonstrating that *Penn's Treaty* is more deeply entrenched in the political and economic situation of the late eighteenth century than in the actual occurrences of the late seventeenth century. Commissioned in late 1770 or early 1771 by William Penn's son Thomas Penn (1702–1775), or perhaps his wife, Juliana Penn (1729–1801), as a tribute to his late father, the painting defended the rights of the Penn family when Benjamin Franklin (1706–1790) and the Quaker-dominated Pennsylvania Assembly sought to dissolve Pennsylvania's proprietary government. The painting, therefore, served to reassert the Penn family's hereditary claim to Pennsylvania and rewrite Thomas Penn's own history of unethical dealings with the Lenape. Indeed, after Thomas Penn died in 1775, his wife Juliana sent copies of the John Hall engraving after the painting to Penn's appointees in Pennsylvania in memory of their service to her husband, demonstrating its role in glorifying the Penn family legacy.[1] The commission was mutually beneficial for both patron and artist as West was, at the time, on the rise as one of the preeminent painters in London. Born in Springfield, Pennsylvania, West moved to the British capital in 1763. He gained notoriety with his painting *The Death of General Wolfe* (Fig. 3), which applied the conventions of grand history painting to a near-contemporary

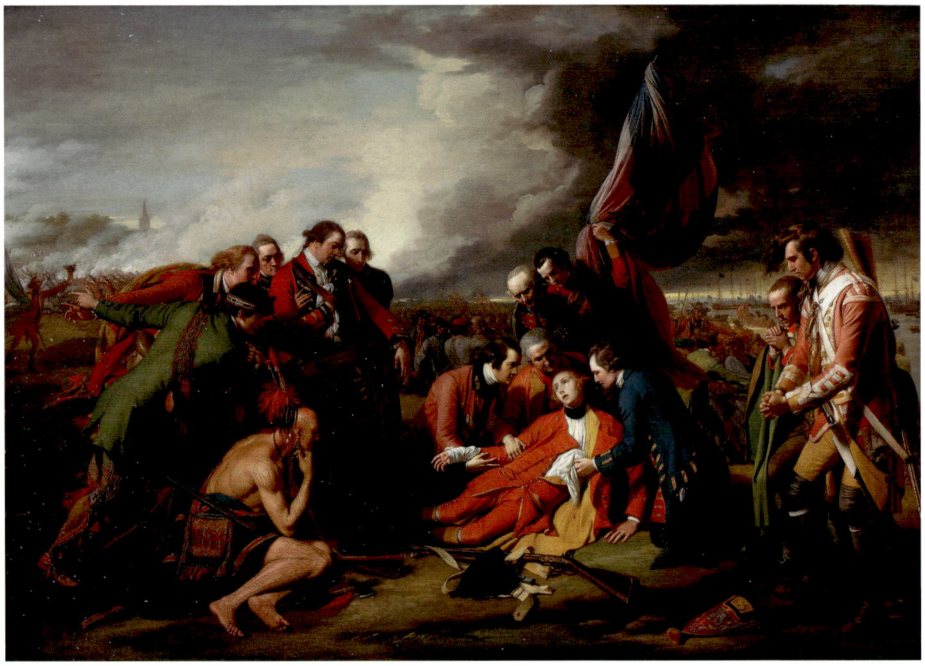

FIG. 3 Benjamin West, *The Death of General Wolfe*, 1770. Oil on canvas, 59 × 84 inches. Gift of the 2nd Duke of Westminster to the Canadian War Memorials, 1918; Transfer from the Canadian War Memorials, 1921. National Gallery of Ontario, Ottawa. Photo: NGC

FIG. 4 Artist Unknown (Lenape), *Wampum Belt*, 1680–1720. Shell, beads, and leather, 6 × 34 × ¼ inches. © Philadelphia History Museum at the Atwater Kent / Courtesy of Historical Society of Pennsylvania Collection / Bridgeman Images

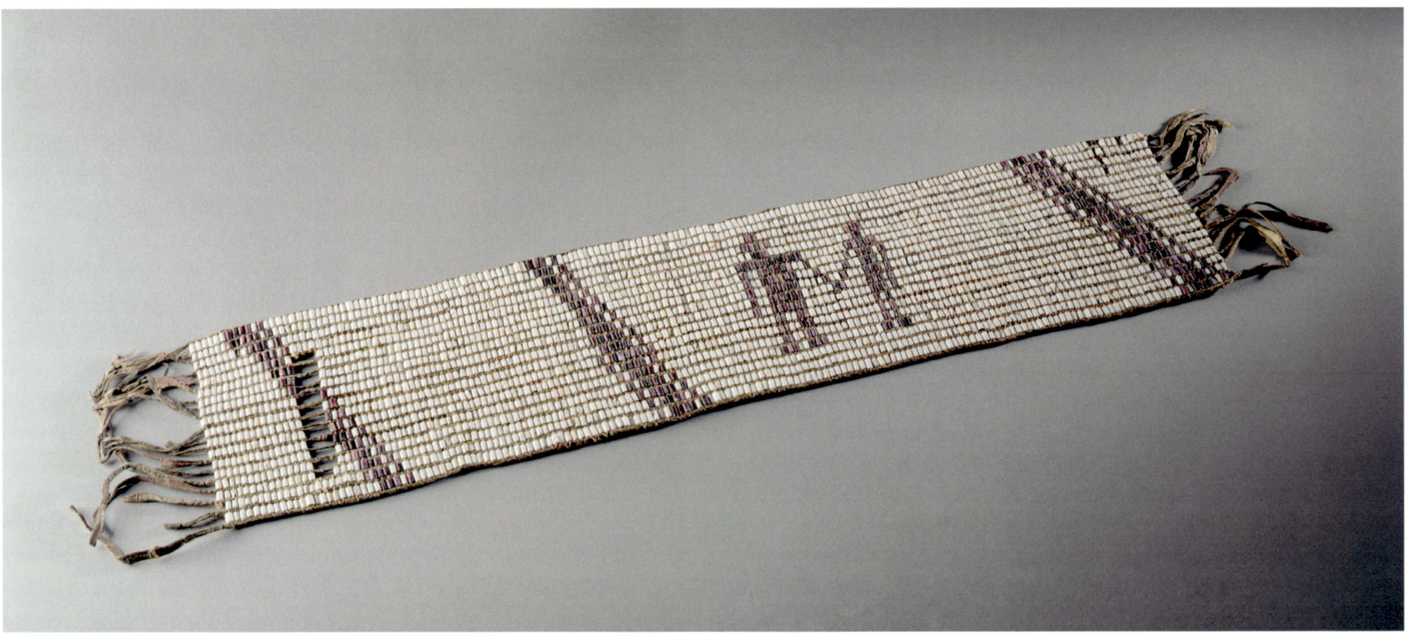

event with figures in modern dress. Soon after he completed *Penn's Treaty*, West was appointed historical painter to the royal court of King George III.

The facts of William Penn's treaty with the Lenape, also known as the Treaty of Shackamaxon, are murky at best. Scholars have long debated when and where the event took place—if it did in fact occur—and even what the contents of the treaty were.[2] The Lenape wove wampum, or carved shell beads, into belts to serve as material records of alliances and intercultural understandings. The belts' patterns, pictographic figures, and abstract symbols signaled specific meanings. An extant wampum belt depicting two figures on a field of white shells is believed to record the agreement between Penn and the Lenape (Fig. 4).[3] No unfurling scroll of terms as depicted by West, however, exists, but it is generally accepted that Penn and his agents conducted several meetings with Tamanend (ca. 1625–ca. 1701) and other Lenape sachems, or chiefs, in the Pennsylvania colony in 1682 and 1683. In 1733, the French writer and philosopher Voltaire (1694–1778) described Penn's agreement with the Lenape as "the only treaty between those people and the Christians that was not ratified by an oath and was never infring'd," referring to a Quaker belief that binding an agreement under oath lessened obligations to be honest in everyday dealings.[4] Not all Lenape agreed, however, that Penn was fair or honest in his agreements. In 1684, Nicholas More (d. 1689), the first chief justice of the province of Pennsylvania, wrote to Penn claiming, "the Indians are Mutch displeased at our English settling upon their Land, and seeme to Threaten us, saying that William Penn hath deceived them not payeing for what he bought of them."[5] West's *Penn's Treaty* omits any tensions or disagreement in its imagination of a peaceful exchange.

When creating *Penn's Treaty*, West drew from a variety of sources, including classical iconography and his own biography. With his visage modeled after a popular eighteenth-century portrait by Silvanus Bevan (1691–1765), Penn is depicted as much older than he would have been in 1682. The tradesmen and Quakers in the painting, two of which are portraits of West's father and half-brother, are depicted in modern-day, eighteenth-century dress.[6] The Lenape themselves appear in classical poses inspired by Roman statuary, and they wear an assortment of Native American clothing and accessories that West had in his studio or borrowed from friends.[7] In his letters and biography, the painter positioned his encounters with Native Americans during his youth in Pennsylvania as part of an "extensive scale in human progress" from "participating in the amusements of the Wigwoms of American savages" to "the refinements of the Royal Palaces of Europe."[8] West's inclusion of items from his collection of Native American material culture in his paintings therefore served to give a false impression of accuracy and cement his own carefully crafted history.

West's painting provided a concrete, visual narrative for the Treaty of Shackamaxon, granting it a revival in the late eighteenth and early nineteenth centuries as the young United States was seeking its own creation myth. As historian Andrew Newman has explained, *Penn's Treaty* substituted a tableau for a historical narrative, "exercising the power of a composed image over a verbal account that was, to use a visual metaphor, sketchy."[9] Prior to West's composition, visualizations of the treaty were scarce. In one such example, the Richardson Medal (Fig. 5), commissioned by the Friendly Association, a group of Pennsylvania Quakers that mediated

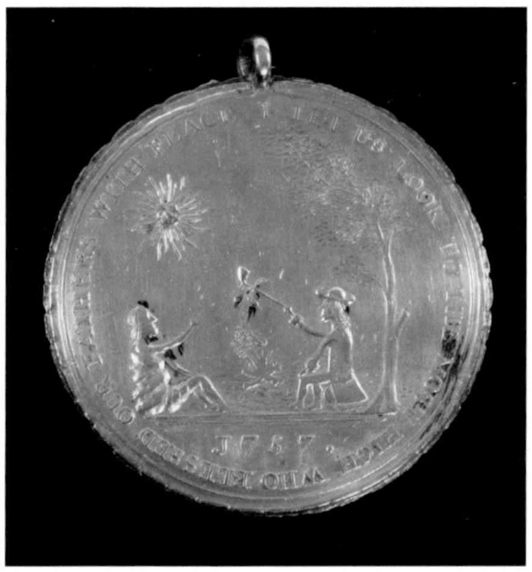

FIG. 5 Edward Duffield and Joseph Richardson, *Peace Medal (from the Friendly Association for Regaining and Preserving Peace with the Indians)*, reverse, 1757. Silver. Library Company of Philadelphia

negotiation between the Lenape and the Pennsylvania Assembly, features a Quaker and a Native American smoking a peace pipe at a council fire beneath a tree.[10] West's painting instead foregrounded the exchange of goods—cloth—for land, as represented by the unfurling scroll.[11] While West portrays Penn and the treaty document in shadow, the parchment is much clearer in the Hall and Boydell engraving, which may either be a conscious decision on the part of the engraver or a result of the medium itself, which accentuates legibility in black and white. The treaty or agreement of peace, initially visualized as the sharing of a pipe on the Richardson medal, was transformed by West's composition into a transaction or sale. According to art historian Anne Cannon Palumbo, West may have meant for *Penn's Treaty* to serve as a call for peace, fairness, and mutual respect between American colonists and the British in 1772, when it was believed war could still be avoided.[12] As the artist himself ambiguously explained, "the great object I had in forming that composition was to express savages brought into harmony and peace by justice and benevolence, by not withholding them from what was their right, and giving to them what they were in want of," perhaps implying that the British should treat the American colonists as Penn had treated the Lenape.[13]

Another implicit goal of *Penn's Treaty* imagery is to firmly place the Lenape in the historical past. The Lenape of West's image are visually anchored to a wilderness that had long been cultivated in eastern Pennsylvania by the 1770s, when the artist began his painting. While the white merchants in *Penn's Treaty* are placed near the Delaware River, which links them to the Atlantic Ocean and Europe, from which their goods originated, the Lenape are resolutely earthbound. Behind the nursing mother stand other Lenape figures, including a group almost completely obscured by the shadow of a tall tree. The Quakers and British merchants are clearly associated with the mobility of the ocean, the transformation of the landscape through development and construction, and the manufacture and dissemination of products of industry, visualized by the crates and bolts of cloth. The Lenape, however, are connected to the dark wilderness that recedes to the right of the scene.

For the painting's European American audience, the image depicts the colonists' right to the land as secure by presenting them as more capable of utilizing and transforming the land, illuminating a fundamental difference in European and Lenape perceptions of land ownership. The Lenape conceived of property rights in terms of active use for specific purposes rather than static possession in perpetuity. In their early land transactions with Swedish, Dutch, and English colonists, the Lenape thought they were merely allowing settlers to farm, hunt, and build houses on land that they would still have access to. Europeans saw uncultivated land as wasteful; provincial law in seventeenth-century Pennsylvania stated that if settlers did not improve their property within three years, the land reverted to the proprietor. To the colonists' eyes, Lenape camps only approximated the European definition of occupied land.[14]

By the time West painted *Penn's Treaty*, colonists had effectively forced the Lenape out of Pennsylvania, first displacing them north to the Susquehanna River and then west to Ohio. In the infamous Walking Purchase of 1737, Penn's heirs confiscated 1.2 million acres west of the Delaware River. Penn's son's Thomas and John Penn (1700–1746), who were then the colony's proprietors, conspired to gain title to land they had already begun to sell to new settlers. They coerced the Lenape sachems Nutimus, Lappawinsoe, Manawkyhicokn, and Tishcohan to confirm an incomplete deed from 1686 that stipulated the transfer of land measured by a walk of one and half days. After clearing a path in advance, three fast runners sped from modern-day Wrightstown to Jim Thorpe, Pennsylvania, traveling sixty-four miles in eighteen hours and covering much more territory than the sachems had anticipated.[15] After 1750, the gradual withdrawal of the French and British military from Indian affairs led to increased instances of colonists grabbing land from and massacring the Lenape. In 1756, Pennsylvania colonial governor Robert Morris declared a scalp bounty, promising money for the scalps of Lenape men, women, and children, and in 1758, the Treaty of Easton required the Lenape to move westward out of present-day New York and New Jersey and into western Pennsylvania and Ohio.[16] In an essay on the forced removals of the Lenape, Curtis Zunigha explained, "Our ancestors' centuries-long, spiritual relationship with our Earth Mother, our Turtle Island, was denied us. Our ceremonial grounds, sacred sites, and the buried bones of our ancestors were all taken by the forced relocation of the Original People."[17] West's *Penn's Treaty*, however, elided this fraught history with an image of a peaceful exchange and retreat.

Myth-Making across Media

Since West's painting was only briefly exhibited at the Royal Academy in London before moving to the Penn family country estate in Buckinghamshire, most Europeans and Anglo-Americans encountered the composition through printed media. While West's *Penn's Treaty* was completed in 1772, the Hall engraving was published by Boydell in June 1775, two months after the battles of Lexington and Concord marked the start of the American Revolutionary War. The *Penn's Treaty* engraving and subsequent printed objects were therefore widely consumed in a different political climate than the one in which the original painting was created, as the newly formed United States sought its own palatable foundational histories.

Margaret Ansell, a British artist and instructor at a boarding school in Tottenham, London, may have consulted both the original painting and the engraving when creating her needlework picture of the scene (Plate 9) in 1776. While Ansell's *Penn's Treaty* replicates the reversed orientation of the Hall and Boydell engraving, her color choice closely follows that of the original painting and her layered stitches of dyed, worsted wool yarn create the appearance of three-dimensionality, suggesting a close study of West's painting and his modeling of forms. Ansell was familiar with West's work; she exhibited a needlework picture of *The Death of General Wolfe* with her *Penn's Treaty* at the 1776 Society of Artists exhibition in London. Ansell's decision to copy two paintings of North American subjects by a North American artist in 1776, when the relationship between the American colonies and the British Empire was at a breaking point, could be read as a political statement, although Ansell's sympathies are unclear. Engravings after both West paintings were also displayed in the same exhibition, demonstrating the widespread and repeated appearance of these scenes so soon after the original paintings were completed, despite, or because of, their political relevance.[18]

While Ansell's needlework and the Hall and Boydell engraving replicated the *Penn's Treaty* composition singularly, and, like the original painting, could be framed and hung on a wall, fine china and textiles reproduced the image in multiples that were sometimes hidden or revealed during usage. A hanging bed curtain (Plate 10) printed with repeated scenes of *Penn's Treaty* suspended atop one another like floating, narrative islands would have been legible when the curtains were drawn shut. When the curtains were opened, however, and tied back at the end of the bed, the scenes would have collapsed into one another, creating an indistinct blur of pattern. Likewise, a saucer (Plate 12) featuring *Penn's Treaty* would be alternately uncovered and then obscured as its holder lifted and set down the cup (Plate 11), also adorned with *Penn's Treaty*. As critical theorist Homi K. Bhabha has asserted, cultural difference and stereotypes are dependent upon this kind of fixity and repetition.[19] The image and messages of *Penn's Treaty* became almost mundane, so pervasive and so widely accepted in American visual culture as to become background noise.

A Peaceable Kingdom

Perhaps no one appropriated the imagery of *Penn's Treaty* more than the Bucks County, Pennsylvania, painter Edward Hicks. Trained as a coach and sign painter, Hicks used his easel paintings to visually explore and express his religious beliefs and engage in ongoing debates in the Quaker community, where he served as a minister. Hicks believed that William Penn exemplified spiritual freedom as the foundation of civil liberty and he produced approximately fifteen paintings of *Penn's Treaty* (Plates 15–17) after the Hall and Boydell engraving and incorporated the scene into many of his iconic, *Peaceable Kingdom* works (Plate 18). When composing his paintings, Hicks combined imagery from both religious and secular texts and sources, creating a rich collage of visual references that period viewers of his work would likely have recognized. Hicks's visual choices in his adaptation of West's original painting also further relegated the Lenape to the historical past and positioned them as passive participants in treaty negotiations in order to amplify Quaker values.

Penn's Treaty embodied the ideals of peace and spiritual independence that Hicks promoted in his sermons and demonstrated the effectiveness of pacifism and justice in political and economic negotiations. He included small versions of *Penn's Treaty* in his *Peaceable Kingdom* paintings, which illustrated a passage from the biblical book of Isaiah: "The wolf shall dwell with the lamb, and the leopard shall lie down with the kid; and the calf and the young lion and the fatling together; and a little child shall lead them."[20] The Peaceable Kingdom paintings were so significant to Hicks and his identity as an artist that his cousin Thomas Hicks included one in the background in his portrait of Edward (Plate 19). By combining *Penn's Treaty* with Isaiah's *Peaceable Kingdom*, Hicks envisioned West's peaceful gathering of Penn, Quakers, and the Lenape as prefiguring peace during the future reign of Christ, when "the leopard shall lie down with the kid." But his inclusion of *Penn's Treaty* also positions the displacement of the Lenape as preordained and a foundation for Quaker spiritual freedom.

While the scroll held by Benjamin West's Penn is obscured by shadows and undecipherable, Hicks highlighted the document in his compositions, moving it into the light and writing legible text for the imagined agreement: "Penn's Treaty / with the / Indians / For / Pennsylvan . . . / 1681." A version of *Penn's Treaty* at the Philadelphia Museum of Art (Plate 15) even prominently includes signatures by Penn and his agents. Hicks literally wrote a contract for the Treaty of Shackamaxon, even though no such historical document existed. The artist also visually underscored the importance of Penn in this transaction: where West placed Penn to the left and slightly in shadow, making the green-clothed back of the kneeling merchant the visual center point, Hicks moved Penn front and center, giving him brighter clothing and bathing him in light. There is no doubt who the hero of this story is, which even further minimalizes the agency of the Lenape in this negotiation.

A later painting of *Penn's Treaty* by Edward Hicks, attributed to the artist in the last couple of decades, provides a new perspective on the composition. One of Hicks's largest paintings, measuring 35½ × 47¼ inches, this work may have been commissioned for a specific person or use, as was the case for Hicks's largest canvases. Hicks removed the merchant and Lenape figural groupings that bookend the scene in West's painting in order to focus on the central grouping of Penn, his agents, and the Lenape, which appears monumental in scale, nearly filling the canvas. Despite these omissions, this late *Penn's Treaty* is perhaps the most faithful to its original source material. Penn is no longer the central focus and, once again, stands to the right in partial shadow. Hicks also demonstrates a greater modeling and more realistic depiction of his figures than in his other *Penn's Treaty* paintings. Hicks was capable of painting in a more realistic style but frequently chose not to, given Quakerism's skepticism of the visual arts. In his later years, however, he exercised more freedom in his selection of painting subjects and style.[21] This late *Penn's Treaty*, with its large size, monumental, realistically depicted figures, and closer adherence to West's original painting, underscores the significance of this subject to Hicks, personally and spiritually, and to his mid-nineteenth-century patrons.

Forest Chieftains and Their Vanished Tribes

The carefully crafted myth of the Treaty of Shackamaxon circulated throughout the Atlantic World in other forms after 1810, after the elm tree under which it was believed the treaty occurred fell down in a storm in March of that year. Newspapers from Vermont to South Carolina reported the ancient tree's demise. After its fall, the elm's wood was collected and preserved as fragments or converted into various artifacts that were disseminated throughout the nation and even across the Atlantic Ocean to England. A large segment of the tree, for example, found its way to William Penn's grandson, John Penn (1760–1834), in Buckinghamshire, England. An engraving published in an 1822 address of the Outinian Society, founded to celebrate the hundredth anniversary of William Penn's death, depicts a couple admiring a tree branch, or portion of the trunk, in an enclosed space on the Penn estate of Stoke Park as if they were viewing a classical sculpture in a museum (Fig. 6).[22] Most of the salvaged elm wood, however, was transformed into smaller, tangible objects that could be handled and utilized, facilitating a deeper, material connection with the past.

One of the more elaborate and complicated incorporations of wood and imagery associated with the Treaty Elm is a relic box (Plate 20) constructed by the Philadelphia historian and antiquarian John Fanning Watson (1779–1860).[23] According

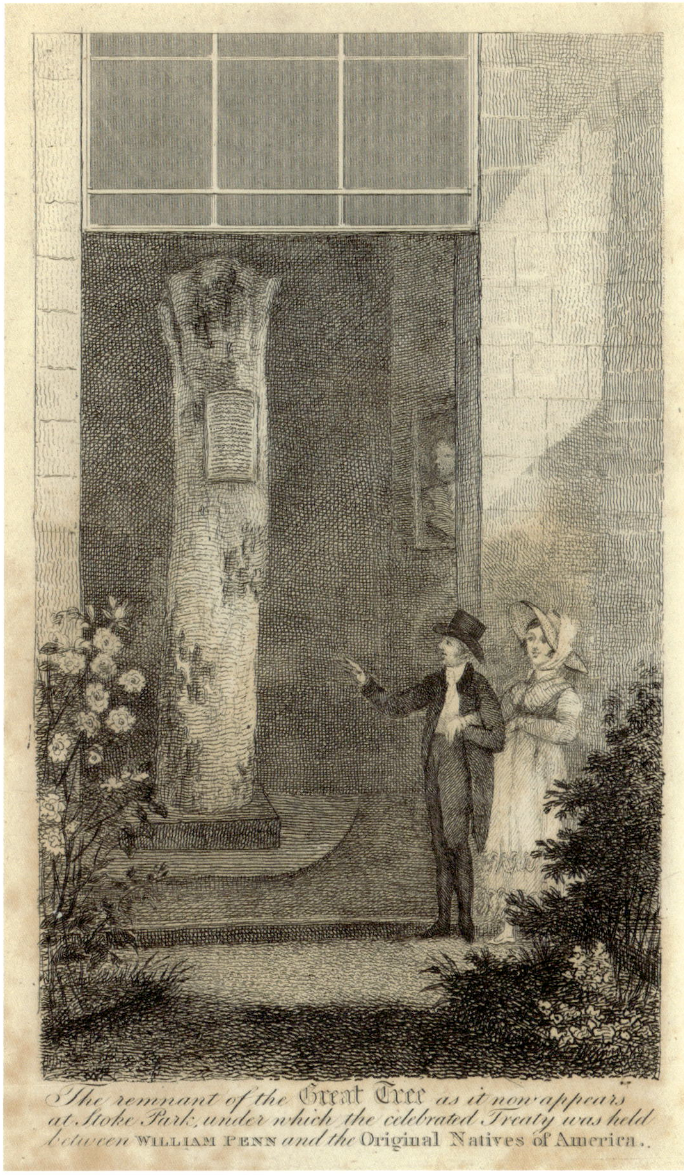

FIG. 6 "The remnant of the Great Tree as it now appears at Stoke Park . . ." from *General Address of the Outinian Lectures*, engraving (London: W. Nicol, 1822), 30. Collection of the Historical Society of Pennsylvania

to a paper label pasted inside the box, it was primarily made from the wood of the Treaty Elm, the walnut border is from a "cluster of forest trees" that stood before Independence Hall, and the small star on the lid and front of the box is mahogany from Christopher Columbus's house. The box, a little over seven inches high and ten inches in width, perches on small, brass animal feet, underscoring the animate qualities of the relic as a whole. Framed under glass inside the lid of the box is a watercolor of the Treaty Elm, painted after an 1800 engraving by William Russell Birch (1755–1834) of the city and port of Philadelphia. The contents of the box span three hundred years, beginning with a twig from a tree under which it was claimed Columbus rested after landing in the Caribbean and ending with a fused group of beads recovered from an 1835 fire in New York City.[24] The box also contains objects identified as Native American. Some, like a portion of "Indian hemp" discovered while constructing the foundation of a prison wall, were unearthed by rapid development in Philadelphia and some, like a pair of arrowheads, may have been sent to Watson as gifts. After the Revolution, as Native Americans like the Lenape became increasingly linked to the past in Anglo-American consciousness, the contemplation of ancient trees like the Treaty Elm provided a means for antiquarians like Watson to conjure up their presence. Watson wrote a poem about the Treaty Elm that conveyed this sentiment:

> But thou, brod Elm! Canst thou tell us nought
> Of forest Chieftains, and their vanish'd tribes?[25]

Watson looked to the elm as a repository of memory of the Lenape, who had been long since forced out of eastern Pennsylvania; thus Watson positioned the elm as a silent witness to the past. Together with the many engravings and objects that bore Benjamin West's vision of *Penn's Treaty*, these relics provided Anglo-Americans a way to look backwards in history with pride in the "harmony and peace by justice and benevolence," as West wrote, that granted them their perceived right to settlement in North America.[26]

Recent work by the contemporary artists featured in the exhibition *Never Broken: Visualizing Lenape Histories* provides a corrective to the passive and receding Lenape figures painted by Benjamin West and Edward Hicks, printed on paper, bed-curtains and china, and denoted as "vanished" by John Fanning Watson. Joe Baker's beadwork and paintings, David L. Haff's paintings, Holly Wilson's sculpture, and Nathan Young's video and sound installation underscore the continuing legacy and evolution of Lenape visual expression and cross-cultural exchange, reassert the agency of their Lenape ancestors, and establish that the Lenape's ties to the area were—unlike Penn's Treaty—never broken.

Notes

1 Juliana Penn visited West's studio in 1764 with William Allen (1704–1780), one of West's patrons and a supporter of Pennsylvania's proprietary government, leading Ann Uhry Abrams and Charles Coleman Sellers to propose that she was the true instigator of the commission. Ann Uhry Abrams, "Benjamin West's Documentation of Colonial History: William Penn's Treaty with the Indians," *The Art Bulletin* 64, no. 1 (March 1982): 47; Charles Coleman Sellers, *Symbols of Peace: William Penn's Treaty with the Indians* (Philadelphia: Pennsylvania Academy of the Fine Arts, 1976), n.p. See also Beth Fowkes Tobin, *Picturing Imperial Power: Colonial Subjects in Eighteenth-Century British Painting* (Durham, NC: Duke University Press, 1999), 56–80.

2 Frederick D. Stone, "Penn's Treaty with the Indians. Did It Take Place in 1682 or 1683?," *The Pennsylvania Magazine of History and Biography* 6, no. 2 (1882): 217–38; Andrew Newman, *On Records: Delaware Indians, Colonists, and the Media of History and Memory* (Lincoln: University of Nebraska Press, 2012), 110–20.

3 Margaret M. Bruchac, "Broken Chains of Custody: Possessing, Dispossessing, and Repossessing Lost Wampum Belts," *Proceedings of the American Philosophical Society* 162, no. 1 (March 2018): 68–71. In later years, objects like pipe tomahawks (Plate 7), were made by European or European American blacksmiths for use in trade negotiations and treaty signings with Native Americans. Tobacco and pipe-smoking play an important role in Lenape ceremonies. A seated Lenape figure in the center of *Penn's Treaty*, for example, holds a smoking pipe. The strange-seeming combination of pipe and tomahawk, a weapon, warns that betraying an offering of peace would be interpreted as an act of violence.

4 Voltaire, *Letters Concerning the English Nation* (London: George Faulkner, 1733), 25. Edward Hicks later paraphrased this statement in his paintings of the Treaty of Shackamaxon. See figure 2.

5 Nicholas More to William Penn, December 1, 1684. From Richard S. Dunn, Mary Maples Dunn, Scott M. Wilds, Richard A. Ryerson, and Jean R. Soderlund, eds., *Papers of William Penn*, vol. 2 (Philadelphia: University of Pennsylvania Press, 1982), 608.

6 Abrams, "Benjamin West's Documentation," 72–73.

7 See Arthur Einhorn and Thomas S. Abler, "Bonnets, Plumes, and Headbands in West's Painting of Penn's Treaty," *American Indian Art Magazine* 21, no. 3 (Summer 1996): 44–53; J. C. H. King, "Woodlands Artifacts from the Studio of Benjamin West, 1738–1820," *American Indian Art Magazine*, Winter 1991, 35–47.

8 Benjamin West to Jonathan Morris, July 20, 1798. Reprinted in Benjamin West, "Letters of Benjamin West," *The Pennsylvania Magazine of History and Biography* 18, no. 2 (1984): 221.

9 Newman, *On Records*, 100.

10 Linda August, "Struck into Metal," Art & Artifacts: Discover the Library Company's Art and Artifact Collection, 2007, http://www.librarycompany.org/artifacts/metal.htm.

11 For an examination of the significance of European-made cloth in Native lives in the eighteenth century, see Laura E. Johnson, "Goods to Clothe Themselves: Native Consumers and Native Images on the Pennsylvania Trading Frontier, 1712–1760," *Winterthur Portfolio* 43, no. 1 (2009): 115–40.

12 Anne Cannon Palumbo. "Averting 'Present Commotions': History as Politics in 'Penn's Treaty,'" *American Art* 9, no. 3 (1995): 29–55, http://www.jstor.org/stable/3109206.

13 Quoted in Palumbo, 48.

14 Joe Baker, Hadrien Coumans, and Chelsea Kimura, "Myth of the Purchase of Manhattan," in *Lenapehoking: An Anthology*, ed. Joe Baker, Hadrien Coumans, and Joel Whitney (New York: The Lenape Center and Brooklyn Public Library, 2022), 31; Thomas J. Sugrue, "The Peopling and Depeopling of Early Pennsylvania: Indians and Colonists, 1680–1720," *The Pennsylvania Magazine of History and Biography* 116, no. 1 (January 1992): 3–31; Michael Dean Mackintosh, "New Sweden, Natives, and Nature," in *Friends and Enemies in Penn's Woods: Indians, Colonists, and the Racial Construction of Pennsylvania*, ed. William Pencak and Daniel K. Richter (University Park: Pennsylvania State University Press, 2004), 3–17; Daniel K. Richter, *Trade, Land, Power: The Struggle for Eastern North America* (Philadelphia: University of Pennsylvania Press, 2013), 155–76.

15 Jean R. Soderland, *Lenape Country: Delaware Valley Society before William Penn* (Philadelphia: University of Pennsylvania Press, 2015), 184–85.

16 Laura Rigal, "Framing the Fabric: A Luddite Reading of Penn's Treaty with the Indians," *American Literary History* 12, no. 3 (October 2000): 571–72. See Joel Whitney's essay in this volume for more information on the forced removal of the Lenape.

17 Curtis Zunigha, "Forced Removals of Lenape: The Original People," in *Lenapehoking: An Anthology*, ed. Joe Baker, Hadrien Coumans, and Joel Whitney, 44.

18 Lea C. Lane, "Freak Pictures? The Needlework Paintings of Margaret Ansell," *Incollect*, November 27, 2017, https://www.incollect.com/articles/winterthur-primer-freak-pictures-the-needlework-paintings-of-margaret-ansell.

19 Homi K. Bhabha, *The Location of Culture* (New York: Routledge, 2004).

20 See Carolyn J. Weekley, *The Kingdoms of Edward Hicks* (Williamsburg, VA: Abby Aldrich Rockefeller Folk Art Center, 1999).

21 This is evident in later works like *James Cornell's Prize Bull*, 1846. Oil on tulip poplar panel. 12 × 16⅛ inches. Abby Aldrich Rockefeller Folk Art Museum. Carolyn J. Weekley, letter to Anthony Seraphin, November 12, 2002; Weekley, *The Kingdoms of Edward Hicks*, 175.

22 Outinian Society, *Records of the Origin and Proceedings of the Outinian Society* (London: W. Nicol, 1822), 30.

23 Deborah Dependahl Waters, "Philadelphia's Boswell: John Fanning Watson," *The Pennsylvania Magazine of History and Biography* 98, no. 1 (January 1974): 44; Yvette R. Piggush, "Fancy History: John Fanning Watson's Relic Box," *Commonplace* 10, no. 1 (October 2009), https://commonplace.online/article/fancy-history.

24 Lois Amorette Dietz, "John Fanning Watson: Looking Ahead with a Backwards Glance" (master's thesis, University of Delaware, 2004), 5; Waters, "Philadelphia's Boswell," 44.

25 John Fanning Watson, *Annals of Philadelphia: Being a Collection of Memoirs, Anecdotes, and Incidents of the City and Its Inhabitants, from the Days of the Pilgrim Founders . . . to Which Is Added an Appendix, Containing Olden Time Researches and Reminiscences of New York City* (Philadelphia: E. L. Carey & A. Hart, 1830), 125.

26 For more on the history, context, and interpretation of Benjamin West's *Penn's Treaty* after it entered the collection of the Pennsylvania Academy of the Fine Arts in 1878, see Christian Ayne Crouch, "Pretty Pictures and the (Re)Framing of America," in *Making American Artists: Stories from the Pennsylvania Academy of the Fine Arts, 1776–1976*, ed. Anna O. Marley (New York: American Federation of the Arts, 2023), 11–19.

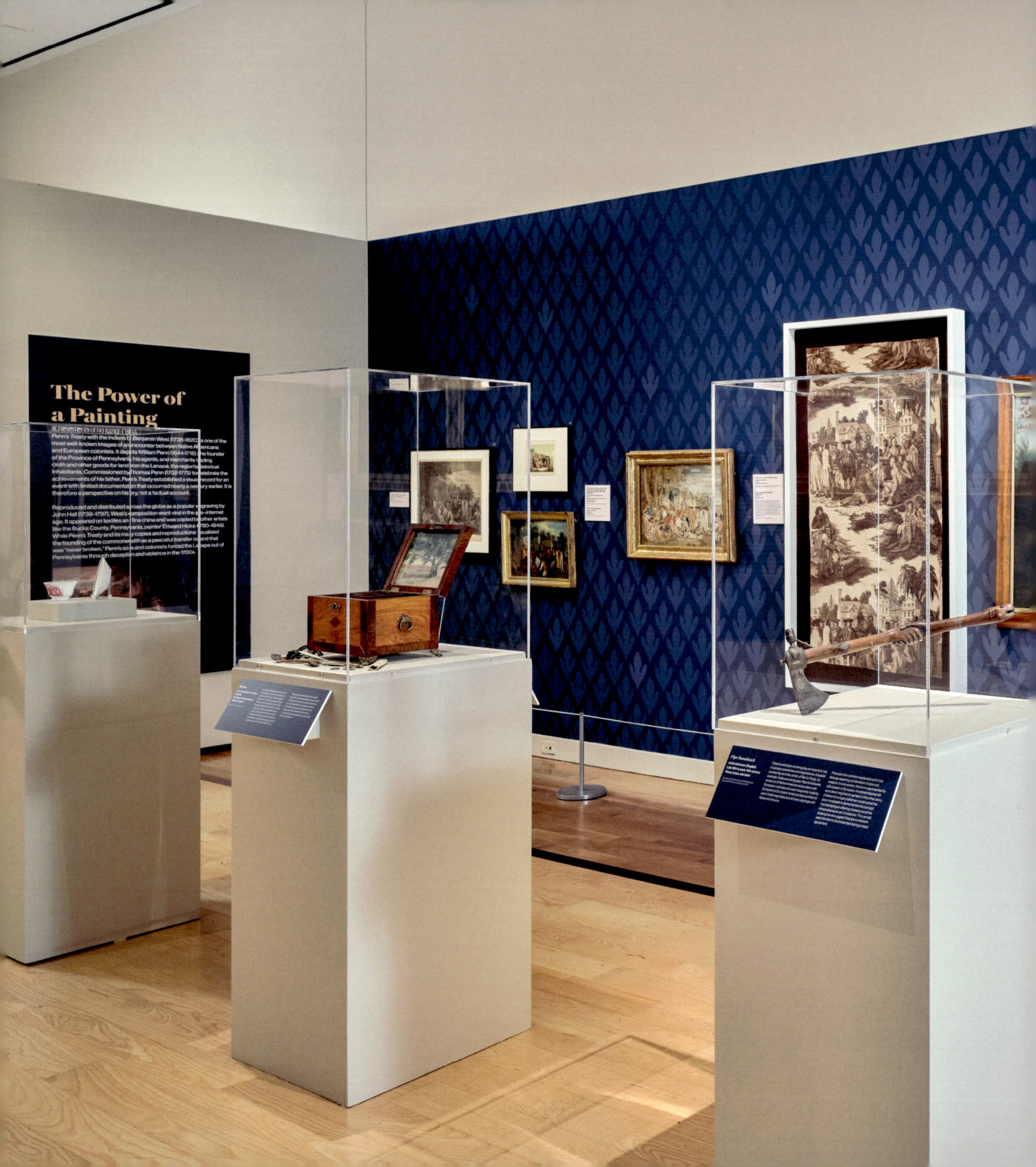
The Power of a Painting
Penn's Treaty with the Indians by Benjamin West
most well-known images of an encounter between Native Americans
and European colonists. It depicts William Penn (1644-1718)
of the Province of Pennsylvania, his agents, and merchants
cloth and other goods for land from the Lenape, the region's
inhabitants. Commissioned by Thomas Penn (1702-1775)
achievements of his father, Penn's Treaty established a visual record for an
event with limited documentation that occurred nearly a century earlier. It is
therefore a perspective on history, not a factual account.
Reproduced and distributed across the globe as a popular engraving by
John Hall (1739–1797), West's composition went viral in the
age. It appeared on textiles and fine china and was copied by other artists
like the Bucks County, Pennsylvania, painter Edward Hicks
While Penn's Treaty and its many copies and reproductions
the founding of the commonwealth as a peaceful transfer
was "never broken," Penn's sons and colonists forced the Lenape out of
Pennsylvania through deception and violence in the 1700s.

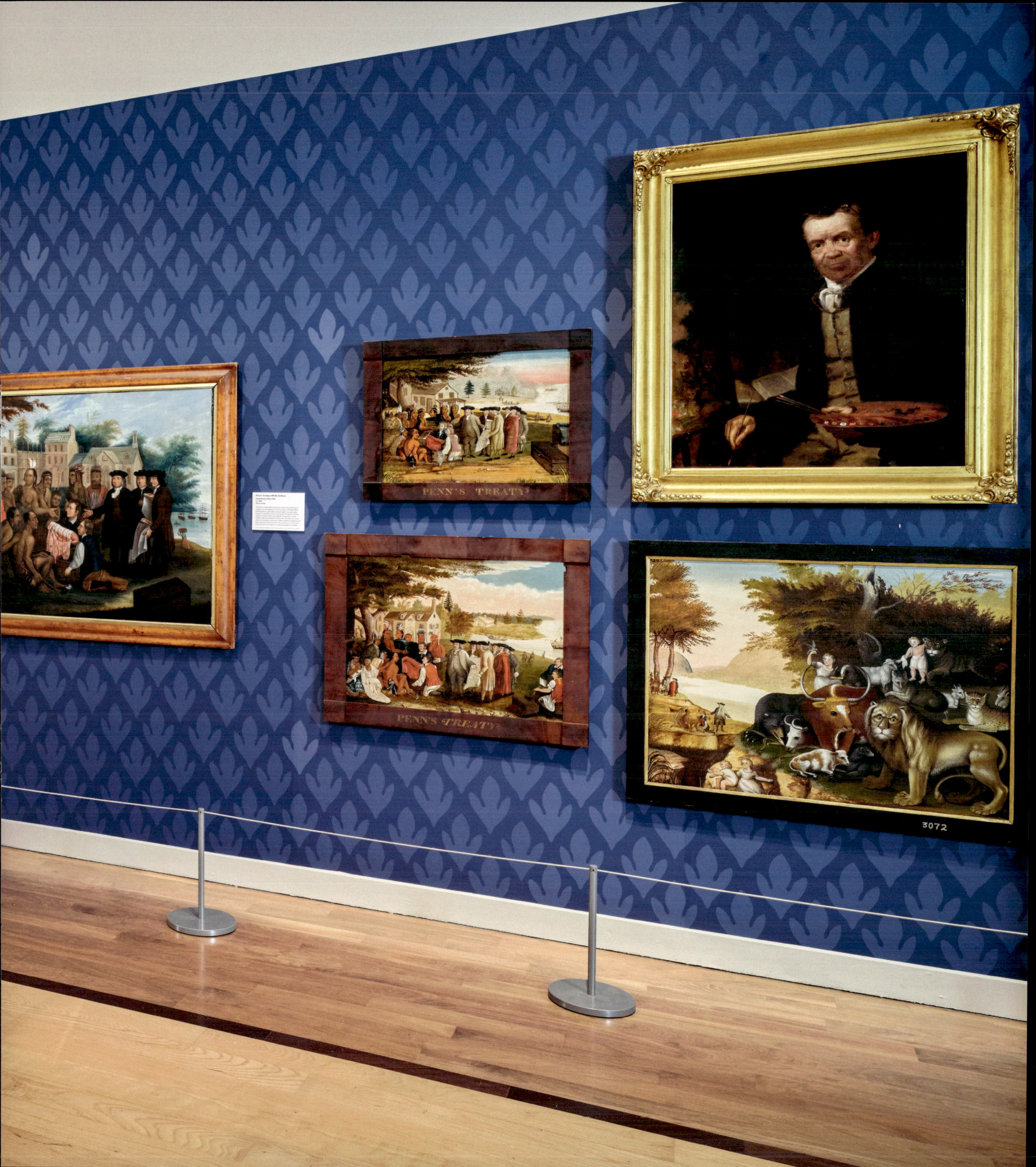
PENN'S TREATY
PENN'S TREATY
3072

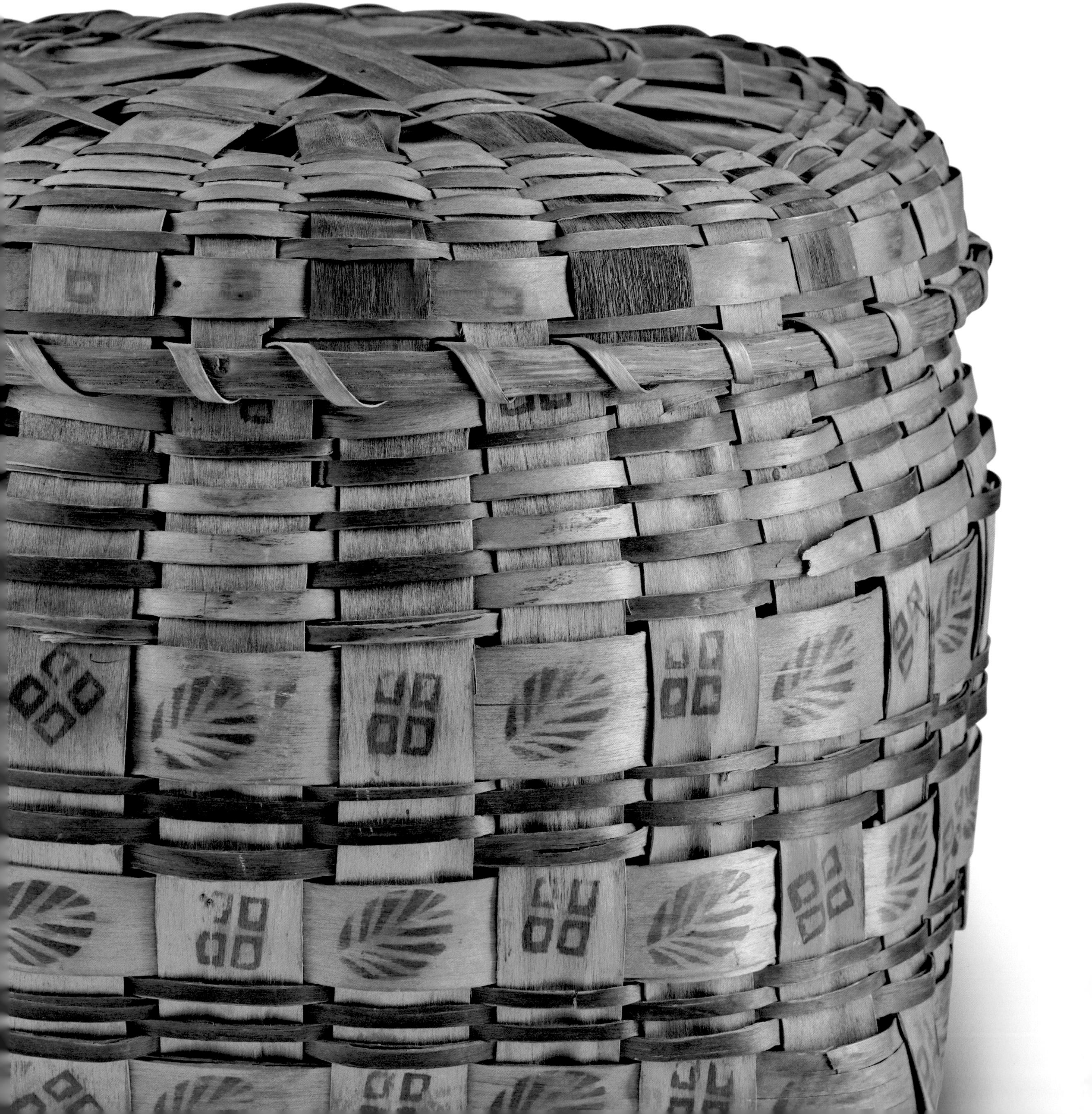

Never Broken

Violence and the Forced Removals of the Lenape

Joel Whitney

Detail of plate 6

FEATURING QUAKER LEADERS IN GREEN AND RUST CLOTHES greeting brightly dressed Lenape leaders under an elm, Benjamin West's *Penn's Treaty with the Indians* (Fig. 1) depicts a mythical event: the 1682 Treaty of Shackamaxon between Lenape leaders and William Penn, whose Quaker family became proprietors of the province of Pennsylvania. This treaty's provisions were supposedly "never broken." During the treaty summit, Lenape Chief Tamanend of the Turtle Clan announced that the Lenape and the English would "live in peace as long as the waters run in the rivers and creeks and as long as the stars and moon endure."[1]

But after Tamanend and Penn forged the treaty, Penn's sons perpetrated one of the most fraudulent and unfair of land swindles, the so-called Walking Purchase of 1737. The painting, commissioned by Penn's son Thomas, availed itself of a fraudulent tradition in Anglo- and Euro-American treaty making, in which treaties were weapons to appease the land's original occupants even as it was taken from them.

But if the budding Americans first stole their land, they also sought to steal the Lenape's past and appropriate their ties to the land. As the new Americans threw off the British yoke, and with it British history and identity, they needed a non-European past, a native story to back up their petition for independence. For European Americans, that story far too often took the form of what Harvard scholar Philip Deloria calls "playing Indian."[2]

As when the Sons of Liberty donned Mohawk garb to dump tea in the Boston Harbor, playing Indian was a way to justify the unjustifiable dispossession: "Kill the Indian and then become the Indian."[3] The 1682 Treaty of Shackamaxon, in other words, was broken in just one generation by the immediate heirs of its English signatory, and its spirit would be violated by many Euro-Americans to come. The truth is it has been continuously broken, never mended. The history is clear. Lenape people living on and off tribal lands today, such as curator Joe Baker and artists Holly Wilson, Ahchipaptunhe (David L. Haff), and Nathan Young—all of whom have work in the *Never Broken: Visualizing Lenape Histories* exhibition—are insisting on historic recognition and justice for past abuses, and a return to their tribal homeland. "We are still here," Lenape cultural leader Curtis Zunigha said. "We have something valuable to bring to the table. We just want to be welcomed back."[4]

The Big House

When he arrived upon the shores of Lenapehoking, the traditional homeland of the Lenape people, Giovanni da Verrazano, an Italian sailing for France, was enthusiastically welcomed. About thirty Lenape, later called the Delaware by the British, rowed out to meet him as his ships arrived in New York Bay in 1524. Nearly a century later, Henry Hudson, a Brit sailing for the Netherlands, was met by a Lenape delegation. The welcome delegation rowed out in dugout canoes, probably made from tulip wood (*mùxulhemënshi* in Lenape). As one of Hudson's crew observed while sailing up the Hudson to Albany, "The people of the country come aboard of us, seeming very glad of our coming, and brought greene tobacco, and gave us of it for knives and beads."[5]

Despite the welcome, little was understood, linguistically or culturally, between the two groups. From Europeans' descriptions, it was clear that Lenapehoking was populated by peaceable people in communities along rivers and streams, that the region was wealthy in coveted furs and beaver pelts, from which Dutch hats could be made, as well as timber and other natural riches. Given that the Dutch West India Company would be established to exploit the region, the clamor for riches blinded settlers to a richer vision; the land's stewards lived in longhouses with unfortified towns, signifying peace and abundance. And they welcomed visitors.[6]

Organized around streams, tributaries, and rivers, Lenape communities were largely autonomous, led by councils whose decisions were enacted by local chiefs. Across the region, they lived in freedom and were united by language, land, and history; shared seasonal land usage and other matters of broad concern were overseen by regional chiefs.[7] Members grew corn, hunted game and fish, cultivated and gathered wild crops and fruits. While each community's layout mapped onto natural features, along tributaries for instance, the land was shared between groups whose overlap was seasonal and flexible. The engraved pottery (Plates 1–4) in the exhibition may have been used for cooking, for storage at tribal longhouses, or for hauling food stores to seasonal hunting grounds. (The stamped baskets [Plates 5–6] in the exhibit were made for European use.)

Within a decade of Hudson's arrival, Dutch and other Europeans noted shorelines rich in beach plums and other fruits that had been carried north along Indigenous trade routes. European interlopers reported seeing trees whose presence was a clue: if left uncultivated, beach plums go to shrub. Orchards were everywhere after the Lenape traded with tribal neighbors. Of the orchards, Penn remarked seeing "not an Indian plantation without them."[8]

The spiritual focus was the Big House Ceremony, the *Gamwing*, represented in Joe Baker's painting *The Big House* (Plate 25). This was a twelve-night ritual of singing and dance. With rest periods during the day, the ceremonies took place at night inside a wooden house (*Xingwikaon* in Lenape) with an "oaken centerpost which supported the ridgepole." Upon this post, two large, carved faces represented the *Mesingw* (or Masked Spirit). Each face was painted half-black, half-red, the colors representing duality. One faced east, one west. A post, entitled *Remembrance*, has been created for the exhibition (Plate 36). For the Lenape, the Mesingw was the protector of animals.[9]

Each of the twelve nights addressed different groups. On the fourth night, special songs were sung for hunters. A cedar purification ritual was held on the ninth night, as was a women's vision song. The post that participants encircled embodied the tie between Creator and Earth, connecting people, animals, and the twelve layers of heaven. Throughout, those who had had a childhood vision were given a platform to sing; the ceremony created a space for all in the Lenape cosmology, bringing individual beings into concert with the collective.[10]

As Lenape traditionalist Nora Thompson Dean recalled in an interview, her mother's vision came when her grandmother fell off of her horse during a mother-daughter horse ride. She had died, probably of a heart attack. In the vision, the trees around Dean's grandmother became people, welcoming her to the afterworld and letting her mother know they were there to help with the transition. This was the vision that Dean's mother sang of in her Gamwing ceremony.[11]

The land and the beings on it were part of a greater Lenape vision. Seasonal sharing meant land was not a commodity to be sold in exchange for goods. Instead, it was a resource given by the Creator for life. This meant that when the Lenape placed their mark on deeds of supposed sale with European petitioners, they were agreeing to a use more closely analogous to short-term or seasonal rentals. European obligations on the "sale," such as percentages of crops grown, went unfulfilled. After Europeans claimed deeds of sale, Lenape petitioned for flexibility by continually using their land and by seeking goods originally promised by those to whom they had supposedly signed away occupancy rights.

Pushed West

By the 1620s, the Dutch peppered Lenapehoking with forts, claiming as "New Netherland" an area stretching from Albany, New York, in the north to Delaware in the south and encompassing parts of what are today New York, New Jersey, Pennsylvania, Maryland, Connecticut, and Delaware. Most of this was Lenapehoking. After resources coveted by Europeans such as beaver pelts and other hides dwindled under voracious European demand, settlers began to disrespect and brutalize the Lenape. They trampled Lenape fields, destroying crops, and they even enslaved Lenape people, shipping them abroad to other Dutch holdings for forced labor while pushing other Lenape people west.[12]

Under the Dutch West India Company, established in 1621, the eponymous wall for which Wall Street was named was constructed as part of Fort Amsterdam and intended to keep the Lenape out of the area. The Peach Tree War and Kieft's War suggested that a brutal, exploitative approach to relations with the Lenape was coming to dominate the interactions. Under company director Peter Minuit, fraudulent land agreements were made with the Lenape. Minuit was recalled to Europe for mismanagement and fired from his post, likely for corruption.[13]

Under Director Willem Kieft, appointed through political connections in 1638, the Dutch levied taxes on the Lenape for their presence in their own homeland.[14] Because the colony was costing the Dutch more than was planned, the director was expected to raise money and spend little. With this mindset, Kieft accused the Lenape of stealing settlers' pigs (it was later proved other colonists stole them) and rallied for war against the tribe through a Council of Twelve Men.

This council, created to push for war, pointed out the peaceable ways of the Lenape, reminding Kieft that the whole Dutch enterprise was predicated on beaver pelts that the Lenape traded to the Dutch. Ignoring their warning, Kieft dissolved the council. Massacres and other Dutch attacks soon followed.

At Pavonia, in present-day Hudson, New Jersey, the Dutch killed at least 120 Lenape men, women, and children (possibly as many as three hundred) in a brutal attack justified after Lenape communities gave shelter to Munsee community members. These Munsees had been attacked and sought shelter; Kieft believed it was a buildup to war. One witness recalled Lenape "infants were torn from their mother's breasts and hacked to pieces in the presence of their parents,"

> and pieces thrown into the fire and in the water, and other sucklings, being bound to small boards, were cut, stuck, and pierced, and miserably massacred in a manner to move a heart of stone. Some were thrown into the river, and when the fathers and mothers endeavored to save them, the soldiers would not let them come on land but made both parents and children drown.[15]

In the 1655 Peach Tree War, as settlers named it, the Lenape supposedly retaliated after a Dutch settler shot a Lenape woman for picking a peach on "his" land.[16] It was a perverse policing of the Lenape on their own land, backed up with ongoing settler violence. These wars hurt both groups. In this case, it was the Dutch who fled to Europe to avoid violence instigated by their own side; the Lenape, thus brutalized, had nowhere to go but west.

As Swedish and British colonial outposts encroached on territories supposedly "owned" by the Dutch, the Lenape initially welcomed the newcomers. As they had for the Dutch, the Lenape offered land under terms the Europeans violated. Lenape chief Mattahorn complained that Peter Minuit, fired by the Dutch but returning for the Swedes, never lived up to the provision of a land-use agreement to provide half of the tobacco the Swedes produced as payment for Lenape land.[17] With relations souring between Lenape and Dutch, Kieft, too, was recalled to Holland, as Dutch West India Company holdings were jeopardized by encroaching European rivals and wars instigated against the Lenape.

But throughout the century, the Lenape remained adept negotiators, statesmen, and community advocates. This was so after the English assumed control of the Delaware River valley in the mid-seventeenth century. It was so as European diseases applied yet more pressure on the Lenape, who were pressed into the western parts of their homeland.[18]

Against this backdrop of stubborn peacemaking, Chief Tamanend may have generously agreed to provide land to William Penn for modern-day Philadelphia, an early attempt to meet the many pressures facing the Lenape not with war or competition but with friendship and generosity. He would have done so to maintain relations that might remain "unbroken" *as well as* reciprocal. While the treaty itself has not materialized, a wampum belt gifted to Penn marked such a meeting (Fig. 4). But just thirty-five years later, in the Walking Purchase of 1737, Penn's sons would cheat the Lenape of over a million acres by hiring runners to expand the distance meant by a "walk."

"They make game of us"

From the Lenape viewpoint, Penn may have indeed dealt fairly with the tribe. But no sooner had he returned to England than his sons and others began to traffic in land sales to repay creditors, and the lands they sold "were still owned by the Lenape."[19] As the Delaware Tribe of Indians in Bartlesville, Oklahoma, states on their website:

> In order to convince the Lenape to part with the land, the Penns falsely represented an old, incomplete, unsigned draft of a deed as a legal contract. They told the Lenape that their ancestors some fifty years before had signed this document which stated that the land to be deeded to the Penns was as much as could be covered in a day-and-a-half's walk. Believing that their forefathers had made such an agreement the Lenape leaders agreed to . . . have this area walked off. They thought the whites would take a leisurely walk down an Indian path along the Delaware River. Instead, the Penns hired three of the fastest runners, and had a straight path cleared. Only one of the "walkers" was able to complete the "walk," but he went fifty-five miles.[20]

The Penns gained an area of land nearly the size of Rhode Island through their deceit. Lenape chief Lappawinsoe expressed the tribe's frustration, recalling, "[the white runners] should have walkt along by the River Delaware . . . for a few Miles and then have sat down and smoakt a Pipe, and now and then have shot a Squirrel, and not have kept up the Run . . . all day." Nonetheless,

> the Lenape felt honor-bound to fulfill what they thought their ancestors had agreed to, and thus began their movement westward. The Lenape were given place after place. Each time it was promised by the government that it would be their permanent home, only to have to move again. Their trek, which lasted 130 years, finally brought them to what was known as Indian Territory, now Oklahoma.[21]

Before the French and Indian War, the Lenape fled ongoing pressures of British, French, and Haudenosaunee (or Iroquois) competition. Though they found themselves in a precarious state of protection under their Haudenosaunee rivals, they liked the Susquehanna Valley, where they were removed to. But the Susquehannock were stewards of the valley—and with shifting alliances and the decay of Susquehannock tribal power, the dynamic changed again.

One historian describes how, alongside the French and Indian War, another war of Indian extermination played out, under which there was

> a prefigurative pattern of U.S. annexation and colonization of Indigenous nations across the continent for the following century: a vanguard of farmer-settlers led by seasoned "Indian fighters," calling on authorities/militias of the British colonies, first, and the U.S. government/army later, to defend their settlements, forming the core dynamic of U.S. democracy.[22]

At the dawn of this ongoing war, the French-allied Iroquois revoked the Lenape's land rights, and the Lenape took refuge in the Ohio River region. Signed by Lenape chief Teedyuscung before five hundred Natives, who were joined by English colonial representatives, the 1758 Treaty of Easton was negotiated largely to sue for peace in Pennsylvania and New Jersey. The Walking Purchase had effectively created the state of war and rancor this treaty was meant to address.[23]

Teedyuscung, whose name meant "as far as the wood's edge," was born in what became Trenton, around 1700. Thirty years later, he was driven to what became Northampton County, Pennsylvania. In negotiations for the Treaty of Easton he sought land for the Lenape that would be protected from settler incursion, lamenting that "This very Ground that is under me"—and here he kicked it—"was my . . . Inheritance, and is taken from me by Fraud."[24]

Once the treaty was signed, and Native allies were severed from the French, Teedyuscung was abandoned by the Pennsylvania government. While he slept in his cabin in what became known as the Poconos, an arsonist set fire to it and the Lenape chief perished in the blaze.[25] This anonymous assassination of a chief in 1763 was not unique. It came to represent a shameful pattern as the nation changed hands from British to American control.

"The French and Indian War would later be seen as the trigger for independence of the settler population, in which the distinctly 'American' nation was born," writes one historian. This mythology of nascent Americanism was conveyed in the 1826 novel *The Last of the Mohicans: A Narrative of 1757*, "in which the author—land speculator James Fenimore Cooper—created a usable settler-colonial history" to burnish the heroism of settlers like himself.[26]

But amidst cunning Euro-American epiphanies that the Lenape might be useful during inter-European wars, settlers committed continuous atrocities and all-out war against the Lenape. According to letters found later, the British deliberately introduced European diseases into the Lenape population.[27] Pennsylvania colonial governor Robert Hunter Morris declared a scalp bounty on the Lenape during this period; and although most Lenape had sought to remain neutral throughout the Europeans' territorial skirmishes, resource competition, and outright warfare, the highhandedness and violent tactics of the British pushed them toward French allyship.[28] The argument between joining European wars and remaining neutral became a constant theme in eighteenth-century Lenape tribal discourse.

Rallying nearly all the Eastern tribes including the Lenape to fight the British, in 1763 Ottawa Chief Pontiac described the British treatment of Natives:

> When I visit the English chief and inform him of the death of any of our comrades, instead of lamenting, as our brothers, the French, used to do, they make game of us. If I ask him for anything for our sick, he refuses, and tells us he does not want us, from which it is apparent he seeks our death.[29]

Under the chief's rallying cry, some Lenape agreed to forgo their prized neutrality to join Pontiac's siege of Fort Pitt, hoping to drive out the British and fortify tribal lands. The uprising was unsuccessful. But in the context of settlers' Indian wars that paralleled both the French and Indian War and the War for Independence, the siege proved an astounding show of force, suggesting the power of Indigenous nations when united for justice.

"Beware of such friends as these"

With the French defeat in 1763, the Lenape were increasingly beholden to and restricted by British whims, even as settlers chafed against the same. Under the Treaty of Easton, the tribe agreed under duress to move to the west of Fort Pitt, in the Tuscarawas River Valley in Ohio. Other Lenape groups moved north to Grand River, Ontario, or Munsey, Ontario. Yet with settlers pouring into Lenape land in Ohio, violating the agreement, the main group was once again without protection and vulnerable to losing treaty-protected land.

In the fall of 1774, British governor of Virginia John Murray, the Fourth Earl of Dunmore, "sided with British settlers who wanted land in the Ohio Country (in part because he was himself a land speculator)." In Lord Dunmore's biased view, "no royal policy could prevent settlers' seizure of Indigenous land." When the Shawnee Nation resisted the seizure of Shawnee lands, "Dunmore commissioned 150 Virginia settler-rangers to destroy Shawnee towns, and he mobilized the Virginia militia to invade the Ohio Valley" and, in the language used then, "proceed[ed] directly to their Towns, and . . . destroy[ed] . . . and distress[ed] them in every other way that is possible."[30]

The brutality of Dunmore's War pushed Shawnees to ally with the British against the breakaway settlers in 1777. As attacks mounted between Shawnees and settlers, the settlers increasingly relied on ranger militias:

> Rampaging against combatants and noncombatants alike, the ranger force fell on the staunchly neutral towns of the Delaware Nation, torturing and killing women and children. In one particularly twisted incident, the settler troops slaughtered a Delaware boy who had been bird hunting alone. A near-riot ensued among the troops over who had the right to claim the "honor" of the kill.[31]

Settlers continued to escalate their indiscriminate violence in the Ohio Country, spurring "the most outrageous war crime, which showed that Indigenous conversion to Christianity and pacifism was no protection from genocide."[32] Christian missionaries among besieged Lenape communities in Pennsylvania had seeded three Moravian Indian villages earlier in the century. Fighting had displaced those in one settlement, Gnadenhütten, in eastern Ohio. But the Lenape returned to Gnadenhütten to harvest maize.

In March 1782, a Pennsylvania militia under David Williamson "rounded up the Delawares, telling them they had to evacuate for their own safety." Forty-two Lenape men, twenty Lenape women, and thirty-four Lenape children were searched for weapons. The Pennsylvanians announced that tribal members were to be killed, and they accused the tribal members, with no evidence, of giving "refuge to Delawares who had killed white people" and "stealing the household items and tools they possessed, because such items should only belong to white people."

> Thus condemned, the Lenape members spent the night praying and singing hymns. But in the morning, Williamson's men marched over ninety people in pairs into two houses and methodically slaughtered them. One killer bragged that he personally had bludgeoned fourteen victims with a cooper's mallet, which he had then handed to an accomplice. "My arm fails me," he was said to have announced, "Go on with the work."[33]

Lenape Chief Buckongahelas, describing tribal knowledge of settlers, addressed a group of Christianized Lenape. He had indeed known good white men, he said. But, alas, the good ones were too few to matter. "They do what they please," he cried. "They enslave those who are not of their color, although created by the same Great Spirit who created us." Chief Buckongahelas continued:

> They would make slaves of us if they could, but as they cannot do it, they kill us. There is no faith to be placed in their words. They are not like the Indians, who are only enemies while at war, and are friends in peace. They will say to an Indian: "My friend, my brother" . . . and at the same moment destroy him. . . . Remember that this day I have warned you to beware of such friends as these. I know the Long Knives [the Lenape name for Americans]; they are not to be trusted.[34]

Lenapehoking, the Fourteenth State

With the onset of war between the Americans and British, the Lenape remained split. Netawatwees, chief of the Unami, or the downriver Lenape, pressed for neutrality. Choosing the wrong side could result in retribution. At the same time, Christian Lenape remaining in the Tuscarawas were pressured by the Moravian Church to join the Americans, despite that church's long pacifism. In 1774, White Eyes was elected principal chief. He, too, pressed to keep neutral.

As settler raids pushed some Lenape to ally with the British, it was not an easy decision. In 1781, Captain Pipe, also known as Hopocan, still struggled with the choice well into the war. As he told the British allies:

> You may perhaps think me a fool, for risking my life at your bidding. For it is *your* cause, and not mine . . . and you ought . . . to fight the Long-Knives. . . . You say you love your children, the Indians. . . But . . . who of us can believe that you can love a people of a different color

> from your own; better than those who have a white skin, like yourselves?[35]

On one side, the Christian Lenape favored the Americans in the War for Independence (as did White Eyes's personal leanings). On the other, the "renegade" tribes (the Shawnees, Ottawa, Chippewa, some Munsee/Lenape, Mingoes, and Wyandots) favored the British, and these tribes pressured Lenape community members to join the British-renegade alliance. As Chief White Eyes maintained formal neutrality, some joined the British alliance with these "renegades."

While Captain Pipe wisely feared retribution after a possible American-British peace, Chief Buckongahelas addressed tribal members' fears of murderous settler-American incursion. He enjoined the Christian Lenape to follow him out of American territory "to a secure place!" He warned the Christian Lenape:

> Do not, my friends, covet the land you now hold under cultivation. I will conduct you to a country where your fields shall yield you abundant crops, and where your cattle shall find sufficient pasture; where there is plenty of game; where your women and children, together with yourselves, will live in peace and safety; where no Long-Knife shall ever molest you! . . . I will live between you and them, and not even suffer them to frighten you! There, you can worship your God without fear! . . . if you stay where you now are, one day or another the Long-Knives will, in their usual way, speak fine words to you, and at the same time murder you![36]

By 1778, the Americans were desperate. To seize Fort Detroit, they needed Lenape and tribal allies. The British had courted and secured many such tribal fighters, including Lenape groups. Hoping for the best outcome amidst such shifting pressures, Chief White Eyes signed the 1778 Treaty of Fort Pitt with the new United States. As reparations for territorial losses, the treaty paid the Lenape $10,000 to join the Americans. Quite a sum then, it was insignificant compared to the land's value. Remarkably, the treaty's article 6 proposed:

> And it is further agreed on between the contracting parties . . . to invite any other tribes who have been friends to the interest of the United States, to join the present confederation, and to form a state whereof the [Lenape] nation shall be the head, and have a representation in Congress.[37]

An Indigenous state, led by the Lenape, grandfathers of the Northeastern tribes? This astounding provision was quietly rescinded with Chief White Eyes's murder, most likely by an American militia member in November of that same year.[38] (Chief White Eyes's wife Rachel Doddridge, an adopted Lenape born to American settlers, and their son George Morgan White Eyes, were also murdered.) As with some three hundred other treaties, this astonishing 1778 treaty became little more than a mechanism by which to coerce Lenape allyship and take more of their land, while retaining a semblance of democratic procedure and justice. The murder of White Eyes was covered up to keep the Lenape in the American alliance.

We can only imagine—as Western Shoshone historian Philip Deloria of Harvard University does—how different American history would have been if this treaty, the first Indian treaty signed by the new American government, had been honored.[39] Lenape, not Vermont, would have been the fourteenth state.

A Lenape Saint?

Alongside such strategies as coercing alliances through treaties, the Americans created anti-British propaganda and publicly threw off their European identity, if in mostly symbolic ways. This new identity was symbolized by the relationship with Indigenous people, and in some cases, by dressing up as Indigenous people, the original stewards of this nation.

It is in this context that, at the dawn of the war, Penn's son Thomas, perpetrator of the Walking Purchase swindle, commissioned Benjamin West to glorify a past that had been exceedingly short-lived, that of brotherly dealings between the Lenape and the future Americans. The painting was finished around 1772, its sentiments striking a chord as

Philadelphia's centenary neared (see Plates 8–17). It may have been a plea for peace on West's part.[40]

In December of the following year, dressed as Mohawks and making the war "whoop" that would become common during American sporting events, the Sons of Liberty sacked a ship carrying tea in Boston Harbor, throwing tons of it into the water. The war for American independence began with patriots donning Indian disguises to symbolize a new identity and a false past. In lieu of an authentic past pointing back to the United States and not Europe, appropriation of Native garb and myth would become a fixture of American culture, especially in moments of crisis.

Likewise, the image of benign Chief Tamanend became a fixture of appropriation and imitation. As war raged across the states, and the budding government debated what future shape the newly independent United States might take, the first day of May was converted from a European holiday, with dance around a maypole, to an "American" one. It was dubbed Saint Tammany Day, Tammany being one of many forms Chief Tamanend's name took under its American uses, seventy-five years after the chief himself had died. Because he had befriended William Penn and supposedly agreed to lend Lenape land to the creation of what would become one of the hallowed cities of a new nation, the Long Knives made the chief into a symbol , standing for Americanness and independence from Britain.

Bandolier Bags

After the American War of Independence, the chiefs' many warnings continued to ring true, and wars on the land's first peoples continued. With passage of the Northwest Ordinance in 1787, and allied Indians' defeat of General Arthur St. Clair, George Washington ordered a seasoned Indian fighter, General "Mad Anthony" Wayne, to exterminate or remove the Lenape from Eastern Ohio. With the 1795 Treaty of Greenville, the Lenape, now war refugees, were betrayed once again and removed to Western Ohio and ultimately Indiana.[41]

Within a decade, white settlers encroached and the Lenape sought land from friendly tribes in western Indiana. The Miami Indians accommodated the tribe, at a moment of dependence on white leadership and fellow tribes that Lenape cultural leader Curtis Zunigha describes as the Lenape people's lowest historical point.[42]

Preachers enjoined tribal members to become Christian, but many were repulsed by what white Christians had done to the Lenape at Gnadenhütten. Their chiefs warned they could not trust settlers, even as their metals, guns, and other wares made them dependent. Indeed, President Jefferson appointed Mad Anthony Wayne's aide-de-camp, General William Henry Harrison, to drive the tribes out, and Harrison oversaw the destruction of Prophetstown, Indiana, where Shawnee chief Tecumseh and his prophet-brother Tenskatawa lived.

These battles, attacks, massacres, and removals continued through the war of 1812, during which a Lenape chief (Chief Anderson) again argued that the Lenape should remain neutral, while other tribes petitioned the Lenape to join the British to fight encroaching Americans and drive them off Indian land. Although the United States praised Lenape neutrality, the new nation forced the Lenape west into the twenty-fourth state, Missouri.

In 1829, a new treaty removed the Lenape to Kansas, with about one thousand tribal members joining the two-million-acre reservation near Leavenworth, Lawrence, and Kansas City, Kansas. During the Civil War, some Lenape fought in the Union Army but were removed in the name of westward expansion, at the bidding of railroad barons.

Their last treaty with the United States, on July 4, 1866, forced the Lenape to "Indian territory." A year later, the tribe forged a deal with the Cherokee Nation for what would become their tribal seat in Bartlesville, Oklahoma, where Brad KillsCrow is chief today.[43]

The Stockbridge-Munsee-Mohicans were removed to Wisconsin. With the 1934 Franklin Roosevelt–era Indian Reorganization Act, the "Absentee" Delawares relocated from Texas to Western Indian Territory in 1877 and are seated today in Anadarko, Oklahoma, with the Caddo and Wichita Indians.

Two bandolier bags on display in the exhibition (Plates 21–22), made from glass beads and dated to the 1850s, were created by tribal members during treks between Missouri, Kansas, and Oklahoma—a time of severe distress.

Genocidal US policy treated the Lenape, as it treated all the tribes, as impediments to territorial expansion and empire. We know that the US often failed to equip or help the tribes in their treks to new territories. Lenape members would have fled with only the essentials: kernels of corn to be planted in the new homeland, for instance, seeds that might have been kept in such bags as the ones on display—the tokens of survival and creativity during a cruel four hundred years among Euro-Americans, whom the Lenape repeatedly welcomed as brothers and sisters. Of this sordid history, non-Indigenous Americans know next to nothing.

Notes

1 Andrew Newman, "Treaty of Shackamaxon," The Encyclopedia of Greater Philadelphia, 2013, https://philadelphiaencyclopedia.org/essays/treaty-of-shackamaxon-2/.
2 Philip J. Deloria, *Playing Indian* (New Haven: Yale University Press, 1998).
3 Ibid., xi.
4 Kenny Cooper, "'We just want to be welcomed back': The Lenape seek a return home," WHYY, July 30, 2021, https://whyy.org/articles/we-just-want-to-be-welcomed-back-the-lenape-seek-a-return-home.
5 John Fiske, *The Historical Writings of John Fiske: The Dutch and Quaker Colonies in America* (Boston: Houghton, Mifflin, 1902), 103.
6 See Herbert C. Kraft and Marshall Joseph Becker, *The Lenape Indian: A Symposium* (South Orange, NJ: Archaeological Research Center, Seton Hall University, 1984).
7 This was so especially after European violence on the Lenape.
8 Samuel Hazard, *The Register of Pennsylvania* 1, (Philadelphia: W. F. Geddes, 1828), 434.
9 See C. A. Weslager, *The Delaware Indians: A History* (New Brunswick, NJ: Rutgers University Press, 1972).
10 "Interview with Nora Thompson Dean," in *Long Journey Home: Oral Histories of Contemporary Delaware Indians*, ed. James W. Brown and Rita T. Kohn (Bloomington: Indiana University Press, 2007), 62–63.
11 Ibid., 62–63.
12 Joe Baker, Hadrien Coumans, and Chelsea Kimura, "Myth of the Purchase of Manhattan," in *Lenapehoking: An Anthology*, ed. Joe Baker, Hadrien Coumans, and Joel Whitney (New York: The Lenape Center and Brooklyn Public Library, 2022).
13 "For granting privileges" to patroons, is how this online *Encyclopedia Britannica* article describes it: Jeff Wallenfeldt, "Peter Minuit," Encyclopedia Britannica, updated May 28, 2023 , https://www.britannica.com/biography/Peter-Minuit.
14 Weslager, *The Delaware Indians*, 117.
15 Alfred J. Andrea and James H. Overfield, *The Human Record: Sources of Global History, Volume II: Since 1500* (Belmont, CA: Wadsworth, 2012), 99.
16 Sam Van Aken, "Native Fruit Culture," in *Lenapehoking: An Anthology*, ed. Joe Baker, Hadrien Coumans, and Joel Whitney, 71.
17 Weslager, *The Delaware Indians*, 124–25.
18 The British imposed the name Delaware on the Lenape and the valley they came from, to honor Virginia Governor Thomas West, who was designated as Lord de la Warr. The Delaware River was known to the Lenape as Lenapewihittuck Kithanne before the name was anglicized.
19 "The Walking Purchase," Official Web Site of the Delaware Tribe of Indians, June 27, 2013, https://delawaretribe.org/blog/2013/06/27/the-walking-purchase/.
20 Ibid.
21 Ibid.
22 Roxanne Dunbar-Ortiz, *An Indigenous People's History of the United States* (Boston: Beacon Press, 2014), 71.
23 Ibid., 72.
24 J. A. Leo Lemay, *The Life of Benjamin Franklin, Volume 3: Soldier, Scientist, and Politician, 1748–1757* (Philadelphia: University of Pennsylvania Press, 2008), 543.
25 Anthony F. C. Wallace, *King of the Delawares: Teedyuscung: 1700–1763* (Philadelphia: University of Pennsylvania Press, 1949), 258.
26 Dunbar-Ortiz, *An Indigenous People's History of the United States*, 71.
27 Curtis Zunigha, "Forced Removals of the Lenape: The Original People," in *Lenapehoking: An Anthology*, ed. Joe Baker, Hadrien Coumans, and Joel Whitney, 46.
28 The other Europeans, such as the Dutch, declared such a bounty as early as 1641.
29 Robert Blaisdell, ed., *Great Speeches by Native Americans* (Mineola, NY: Dover Publications, 2000), 18; Norman B. Wood, *Lives of Famous American Chiefs from Cofachiqui, the Indian Princess, and Powhatan, down to and including Chief Joseph and Geronimo* (Aurora, IL: American Indian Historical Publishing Company, 1906).
30 Dunbar-Ortiz, *An Indigenous People's History of the United States*, 71–72.
31 Ibid.
32 Ibid.
33 Ibid., 72–73.
34 Ibid., 73–74.
35 Blaisdell, *Great Speeches by Native Americans*, 25; B. B. Thatcher, *Indian Life and Battles: A Minute and Graphic Story of the Early Indian in the United States* (Akron, OH: New Werner, 1910).
36 Blaisdell, *Great Speeches by Native Americans*, 27–28; Thatcher, *Indian Life and Battles*.
37 "Treaty with the Delawares: 1778," The Avalon Project, Yale Law School, accessed June 8, 2023, https://avalon.law.yale.edu/18th_century/del1778.asp.
38 Anthony Gregg Roeber, *Ethnographies and Exchanges: Native Americans, Moravians, and Catholics in Early North America* (State College: Penn State Press, 2010), 10.
39 School for Advanced Research, "Lenape: Imagining the Indigenous States of America, with Philip Deloria," filmed February 18, 2021, https://youtu.be/AGhB5_oJA2s.
40 See Laura Turner Igoe's essay in this volume.
41 Zunigha, "Forced Removals of the Lenape," 52–58.
42 Ibid., 54.
43 Ibid., 52–58.

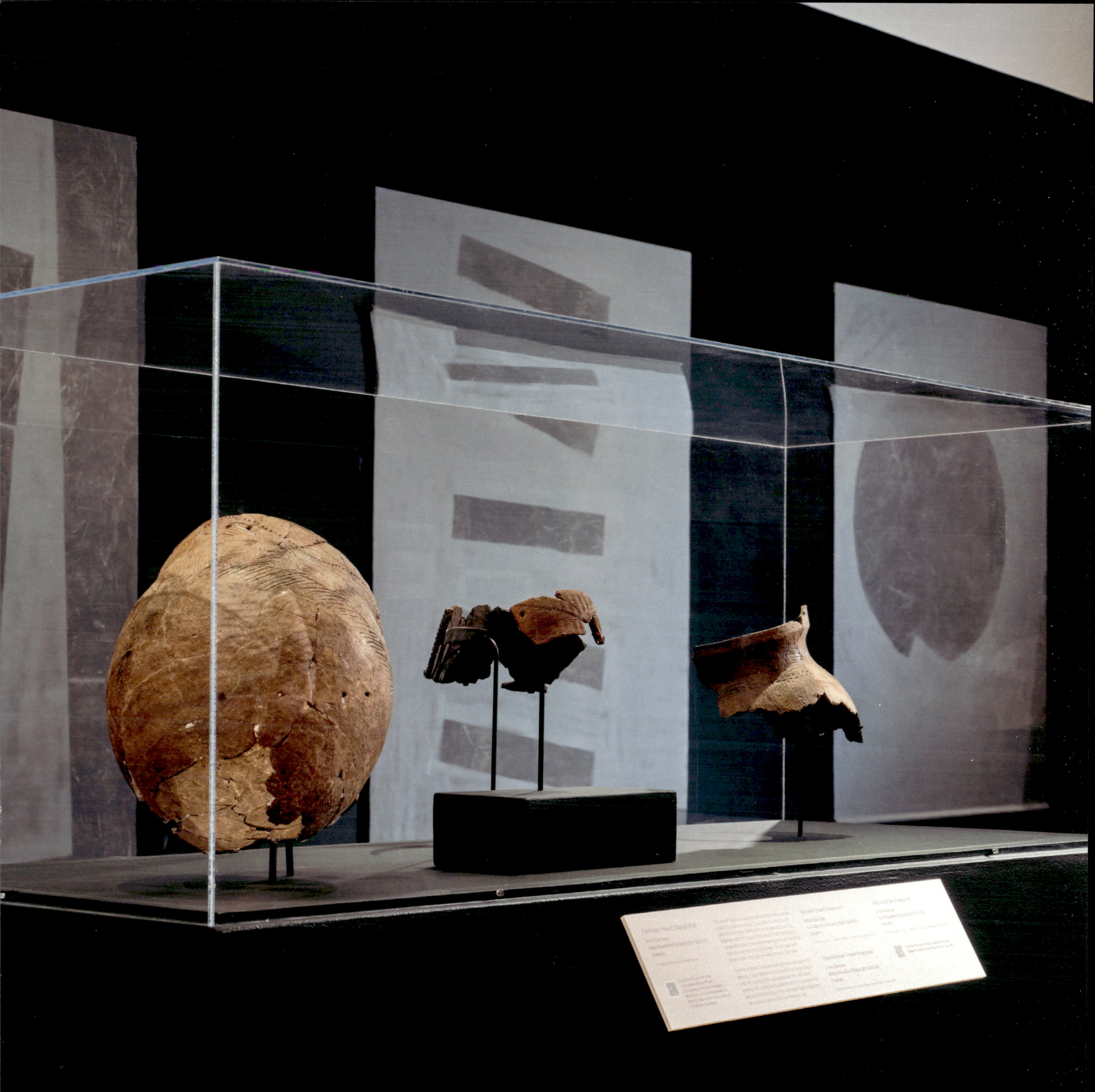

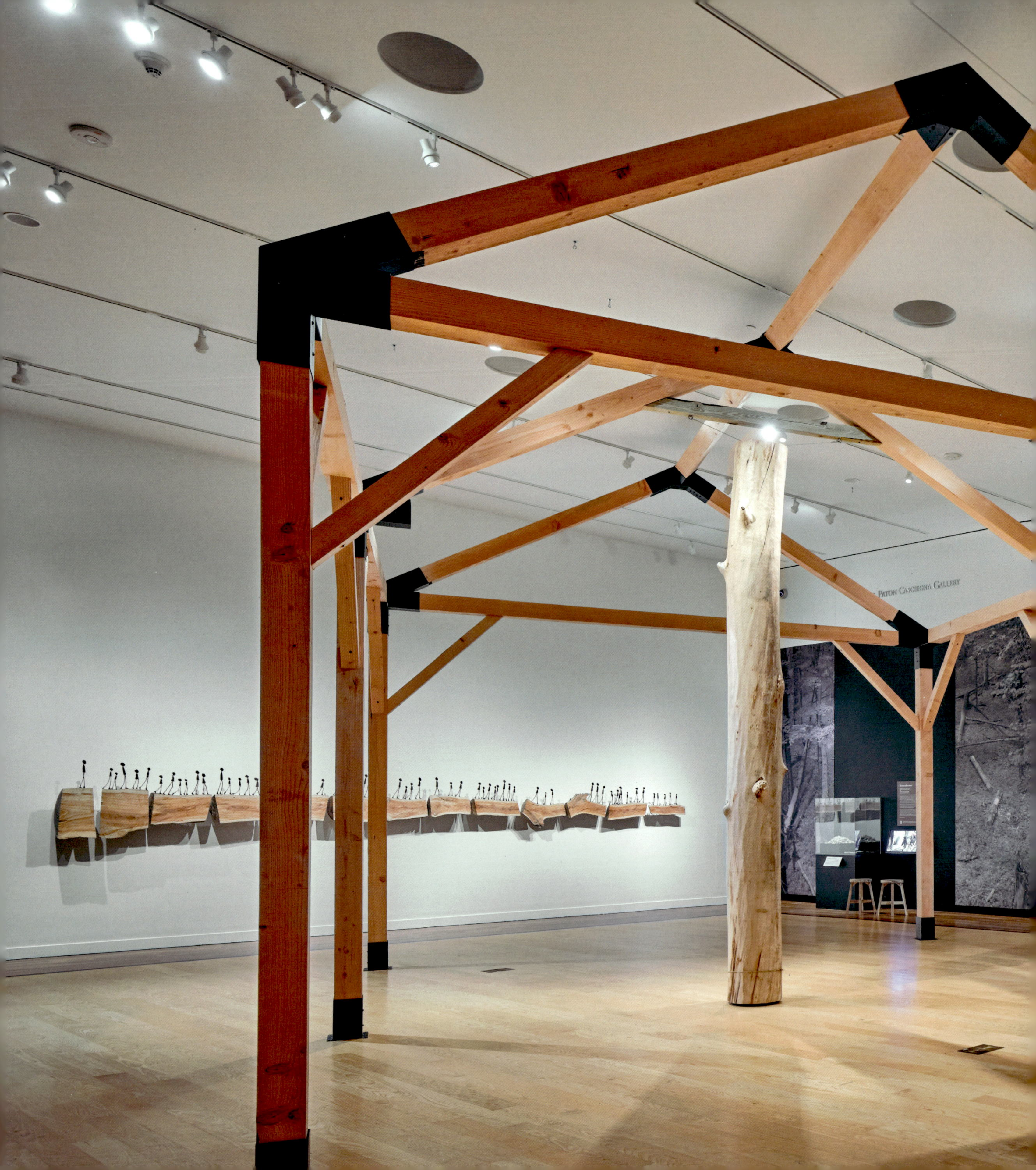

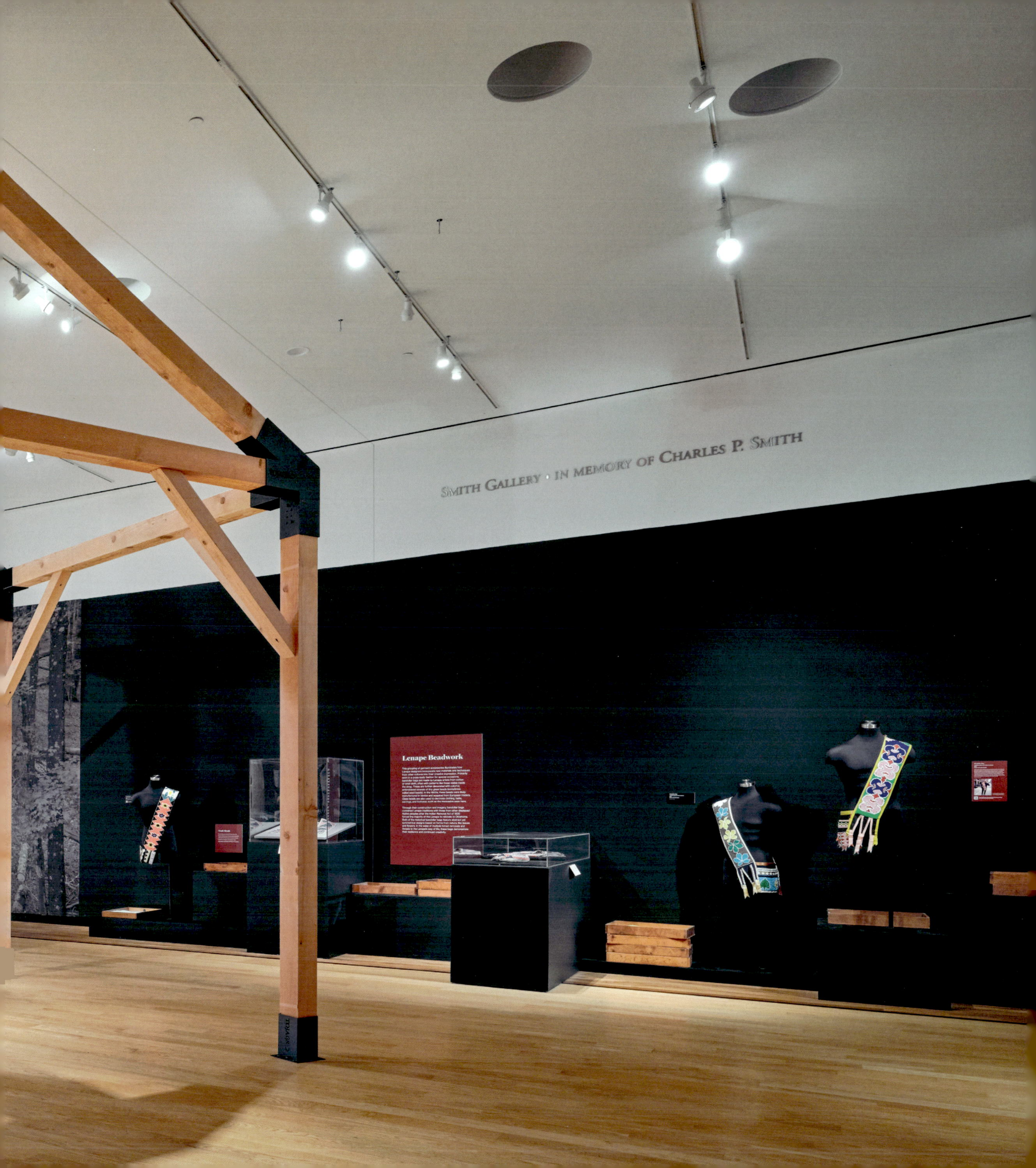
SMITH GALLERY · IN MEMORY OF CHARLES P. SMITH
Lenape Beadwork

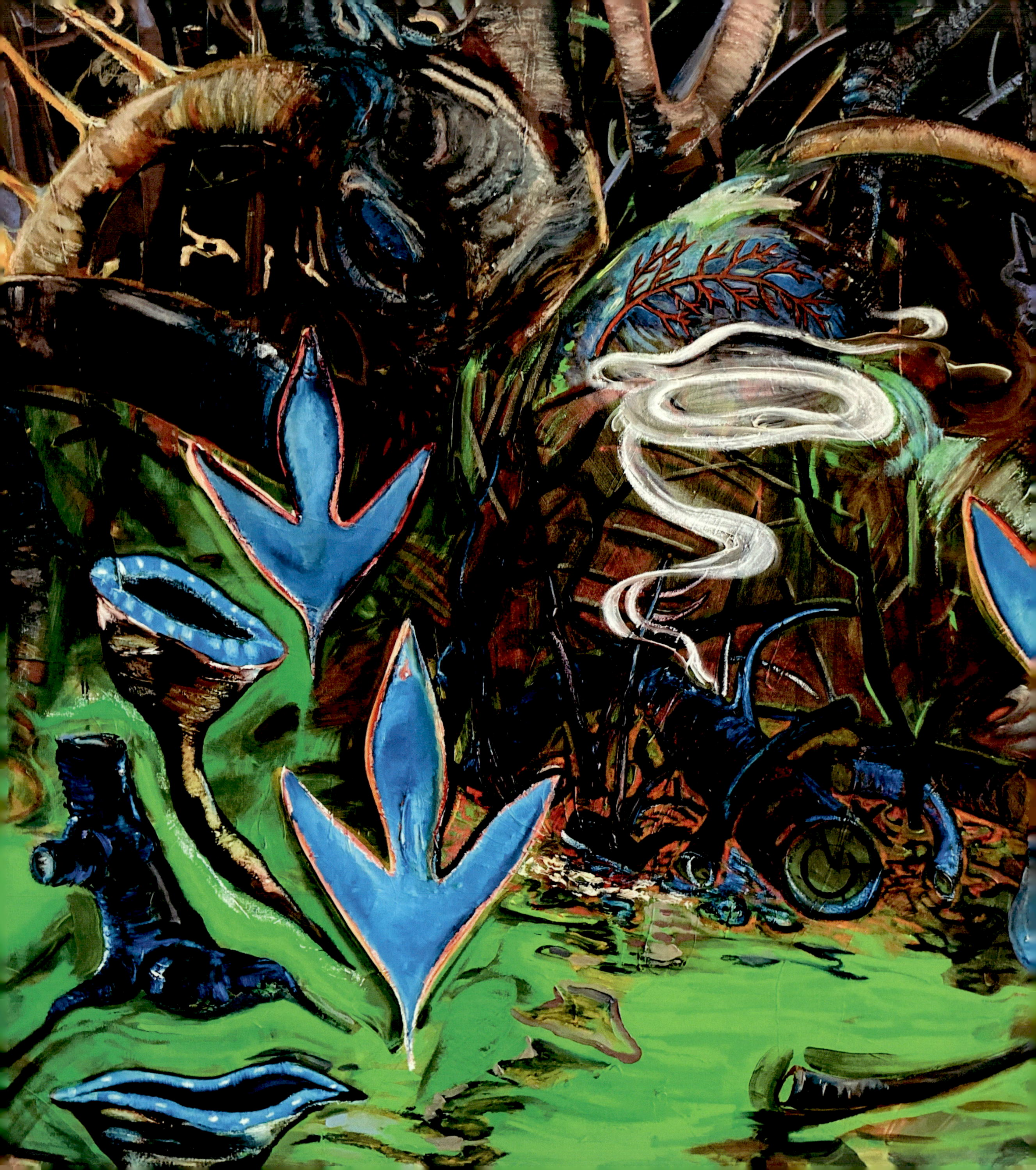

Nèk Elànkumàchi Maehëleyok

The Relatives Gathered

Joe Baker

Detail of plate 24

TWO OF THE *NEVER BROKEN* EXHIBITION'S PARTICIPATING artists (Ahchipaptunhe and Joe Baker) are direct-line descendants of Chief Nutimus (1650–1756), who signed the confirmation deed for the Walking Purchase under protest in 1737, and Tamanend (1625–1701), who negotiated the peace treaty with William Penn in 1682. This ancestry harkens back to the earliest founding of the United States. The American public more commonly hears of the descendants of the *Mayflower* and Henry Hudson, not the Native people who existed for thousands of years before the great interruption and are still here today. All the participating artists in this exhibition employ visual references rooted in memory and land and a telling of stories.

While much of the world seems to be confronting its colonial history, the United States falls behind by continuing to support the idea of a "peaceable kingdom" and the "purchase of Manhattan." This myth-making has an impact on the youngest of our community.

Recently, the Lenape Center collaborated with Columbia University Teachers College students in a course called Indigenous Curriculum and Teaching: Sustaining Survivance through Theory and Practice, taught by Dr. Rachel Talbert, postdoctoral fellow at the Gordon Institute for Urban and Minority Education, to create curriculum centering Lenape sovereignty and survivance for students from prekindergarten to twelfth grade.[1] In the test-taught lessons for young children, it was found that pre-kindergarteners at three and four years old already thought that Indians were gone. This is a common misconception among older students because curricula in schools teach a historic narrative of Indigenous peoples, but it was surprising to see that students with very little school experience already had this idea of the "vanished" Indian.[2]

By creating new work to challenge the myth-making and propaganda of the American experience, the artists in *Never Broken* push back against the ongoing colonial society forced upon Native people. By claiming their rightful inheritance, these artists demonstrate the power of art to create a retelling of the true history of the founding of the United States of America.[3] The Lenape's familial ties to place have never been broken and continue to find expression through artistic practice.

Ahchipaptunhe, David L. Haff (Delaware Tribe of Indians and Cherokee)

David L. Haff presents a series of unbound, loose canvas responses (Plates 32–35) to historic Lenape pottery and basketry in the exhibition (Plates 1–6). Below, the artist comments regarding his approach and process.

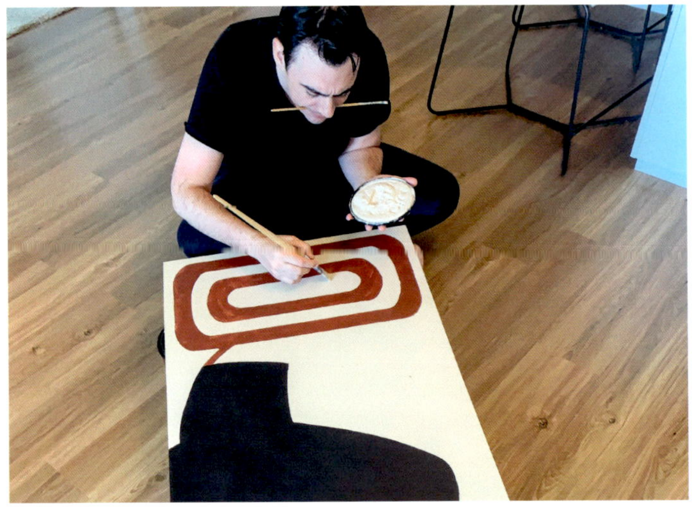

FIG. 7 Ahchipaptunhe (David L. Haff) painting in his studio, 2021. Courtesy of the artist

> A great river flows deep under the rocky lands of the Northeast. It formed the first lakes, rivers, and streams that gave life to all living things in Lenapehoking. Clay formed, reeds emerged from the shores, and life grew abundantly. Lenape hands prepared vessels to bring the great gifts into their homes. Honoring the gifts of Lenapehoking, decorations were applied to pottery and basketry. Hands stamping, carving, and etching across the surface, makers added their forms of gratitude to these sacred vessels in their voices. These visions flood my mind as I look over the worn and broken pieces of my ancestral pottery.

APPROACH

Before materials are collected, nature first leaves its impressions upon them. The texture of clay and the straightness of a reed show these impressions. Artists learned to utilize these natural perfections to enhance their craft. Laying large swaths of primed cotton on the earth, I utilize these same techniques of incorporating nature's perfections into my work. Pushing the paint across the canvas like clay slip leaves cracks, checks, and areas of pooling. While the paint is drying, I begin to impress my geometric forms into the damp surface so that when the paint cures the layers are interwoven.

Seeking to understand the old techniques of mark-making by the Lenape, I diligently carved geometric forms into potatoes and used broken tree limbs and other organic forms to make impressions on paper. As I investigated these processes, I felt connected to something greater than I had first acknowledged. The significance of the marks was not about the beautiful geometry, nor their unique applications, but instead, the fact that each mark was produced by a living, breathing ancestor in our ancient homelands. The smallest of marks had become a river in my heart flowing across time and distance. Each mark is a reminder of gratitude, connection, and the opportunity to leave our impressions for future generations. With loving gratitude to Lenapehoking, may your soil always be rich with clay, and your shores abundant with life.

ART STYLE

There was a time that I refused to call myself a Native artist as that statement often came with certain conclusions or preconceived notions that I wasn't ready to discuss. As I grew in my practice, I recognized that my work resembled that of oral traditions. Using color, form, and space I utilize the engagement as an opportunity to share themes about nativeness in a way that I believe honors my ancestors' traditions, culture, and history in a modern voice. Native modern art to me is about looking beyond and pulling forward all the significance that has become embedded over time. All my favorite oral stories conclude in the same way, abruptly, and without explanation.

Phrases like "and that's just how it was in those days" remind me of abstract art. It allows me to tell a story and grants the experiencer the opportunity to question their relationship to that experience. Oral traditions are stories set in the past while spoken in a contemporary voice, there is a direct connection to those from the past, present, and future. My style seeks to honor the *achimwisàk*, or storytellers, in my artistic voice. A reminder that we are still here, forging paths for a future generation to look upon and see their connections back to Lenapehoking. *Wanishi*, it is done in a good way.[4]

Holly Wilson (Delaware Nation and Cherokee)

In her work *Bloodline* (Plate 31), Holly Wilson explores her family heritage through figuration and storytelling. Inspired by a story told to her by her mother, she goes in search of her ancestral family. Wilson, who works outside of expected American Indian contemporary art practice, utilizes Western techniques of lost wax casting, which can be traced to southern Palestine in 3700 BCE. The process spread around the world, in Europe, the Middle East, and Asia, as well as in Africa and the Americas. Below, the artist speaks about *Bloodline*.

> It is the stories of family, history, and identity that brought me to *Bloodline*. It is a long trail of my Native American history, my bloodline. To be "on the Rolls" as a Native American you must prove a quantum of blood verified through birth and death records until you match up to a name on the official Dawes Rolls. As I began walking through the past to document my blood, with the names and some faces, I wanted to hear them speak and tell their story. I wanted them to be counted.
>
> The figures walk across a locust tree base that came down in a storm. It is cut lengthwise, exposing the rough center, revealing the lines that show its life and history. I de-barked the exterior but kept the curve of the tree and its raw surface. You see the figures walking through time—their life above and the tree's life below.
>
> The Cigar Figures come from a childhood Native American story that my mother told of the "Stick People." The "Stick People" would run through the night and call your name; if you went with them, you were never heard from again. She never described the figures, and I was always drawn to the idea of what they looked like. The Cigar Figures are my reimagining of that story, now a story of family and my past—a complicated narrative of loss, survival, and resilience.
>
> The figures are made from real cigars and found sticks cast in bronze. The faces are of the ancestors from my past as far back as I can trace. There are sections for each generation, beginning with my children. Though I only have two, there are five figures. Each life is counted, and the children who did not survive are remembered with a place on the wood in history; their forms are small, and their heads are bowed.

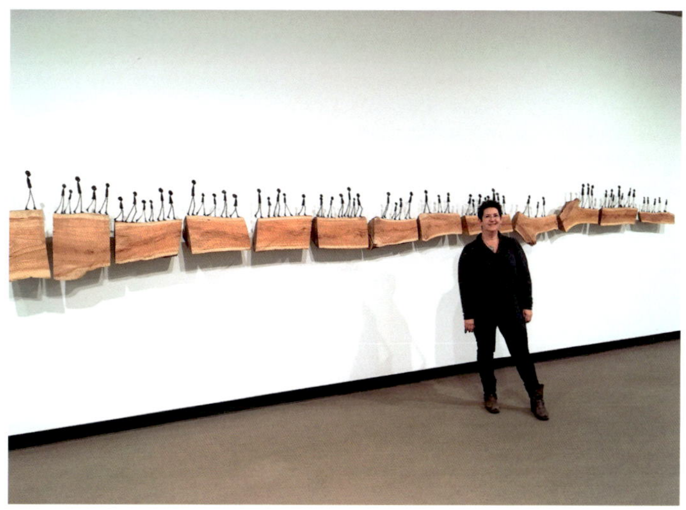

FIG. 8 Holly Wilson with *Bloodline*, 2015. Bronze and locust wood, 29 inches × 22 feet × 9 inches. Courtesy of the artist

Next, I have my section with my sisters and brother, followed by my mother's and father's history weaving back and forth. When hung, the light casts a shadow of the figures on the wall. This shadow represents memory for me. Like a shadow, these memories cannot be held, and in the end, we are all only a shadow in history, shadows on this earth.[5]

Joe Baker (Delaware Tribe of Indians)

My Lenape family has been the foundation of my life's work, beginning when I was a small child on the dance grounds as a member of the Lenape Club, before the creation of the Delaware Powwow in 1963. My understanding of the world was shaped by stories of my Whiteturkey family, my second great-grandfather Simon Whiteturkey, and my great-grandmother Lillie Whiteturkey. I am a direct line descendent of prominent Lenape leaders that include the following:

> Captain Anderson Sarcoxie (1784–1876), my third great-grandfather and a party to the Treaty of Greenville.
>
> Koquethagechton White Eyes (1730–1778), my fourth great-grandfather and a party to the Treaty of Fort Pitt in 1778.
>
> Netawatwees or King Newcomer (1686–1776), my fifth great-grandfather and a party to the Treaty of Conestoga.
>
> Chief Nutimus (English name, Turkey, 1650–1756), my sixth great-grandfather, who signed the confirmation deed for the Walking Purchase under protest.
>
> Tamanend, King Tammany (1628–1701), my seventh great-grandfather and a party to the Treaty of Shackamaxon in 1682 with William Penn.

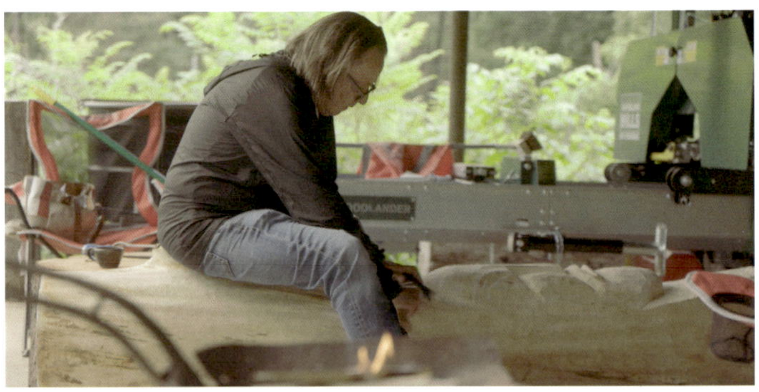

FIG. 9 Joe Baker carving *Remembrance*, 2023. Photo by Marc D'Agostino

Ma Wah Taise, Keeper of the Doll

The Doll Dance ceremony of the Lenape is no longer practiced. The role of Keeper of the Doll is still passed down through families, including my own. Ma Wah Taise's daughter, Akweapailu, Lisey Whiteturkey, died young of tuberculosis in 1894. After her death, it was decided that Sam Whiteturkey's daughter, Phoebe, would be raised to become the next Keeper of the Doll. My grandmother, Stella Whiteturkey Fugate, and her two sisters, Pearl and Bess, danced in the last Doll Dance, which was performed near Copan, Oklahoma, in the early 1900s. Below, I excerpt a previously published article I wrote about my great-aunts Pearl and Bess.

> Two Chevrolet Bel Airs are parked two spaces apart on Main Street. My grandmother's two sisters are distanced by a forty-year silence taken since to the grave. As different as alike, they hold tight some long-ago family secret. Aunt Pearl had certain "Methodist ways." She wore only brown and married but one time, and her hair was pulled back in a tightly held bun. She was forever shading her eyes with her hand. She was polite, but cool. Her white husband was a veteran of World War II and worked the lease on her allotment lands; together they had one son. They lived in a small, unpainted lease house on the eastern edge of the allotment. Her lands wrapped around Stella's to the north and west. Her wells were pumping; ours were not. One late afternoon, we drove out to the land, something Mother liked to do. [We got out and walked around.] It was tornado season. Soon, a greenish-yellow cloud fell over us as the winds

kicked up the trees along the river. Mother looked to the east and said, "Get into the car, now!" My sister and I clambered into the back seat, watching the sky through the back windshield as the car lurched and churned through the earthen ruts toward the gravel section line. No words were spoken, as Mother gripped the steering wheel and turned the car into the driveway at Pearl's place, under the tall locust trees. My sister and I saw the cellar doors just north of the garage. "Wait here," Mother directed as she got out of the car and moved purposefully toward the back. Pearl stepped into the yard, shielding her eyes with her hand, looking toward the car and up at the sky.

Suddenly, Mother turned and bolted toward the car. In one quick motion we were in reverse heading fast toward town. The dust behind shielding the sky. No words were spoken. Aunt Betty wore only one color, had one son, and married five times. She wore Chanel perfume and couture fashions purchased in Kansas City. Her beauty was unchallenged, seductive and misleading. She fought furiously for love, stabbing those who deceived her with the broken ends of beer bottles. Her white veteran husband worked at various jobs. Her allotment lands were gone. She never spoke of Pearl. We walked on Main Street, our silence shaped by unspoken actions long ago. Refugees of U.S. policy, the Allotment Act, pious Christian thought, greed. Our lives were lived always spaces apart, in worlds split by silence. We walked.[6]

Nathan Young IV (Delaware Tribe of Indians, Pawnee, and Kiowa)

Nathan Young's ambitious long-play video installation "walks back" or "reclaims" the pathway of the infamous Walking Purchase, a 1737 land grab perpetrated by the sons of William Penn and Pennsylvania authorities with the aid of the Iroquois, resulting in the loss of 1.2 million acres to the Penn family and the removal of the Lenape from their ancestral land.[7] Young starts his piece at Ottsville, Pennsylvania, where one of the Penns' "walkers," Solomon Jennings, dropped out, and returns to the starting point of the original walk at

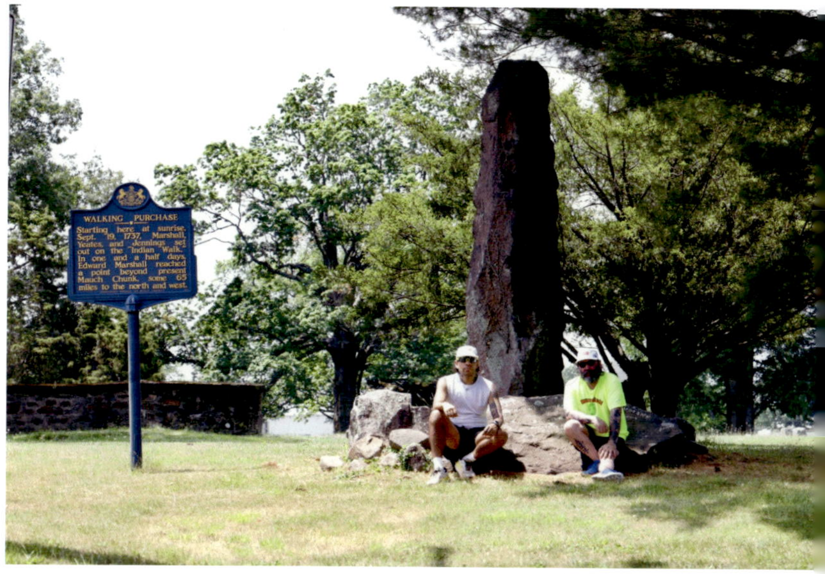

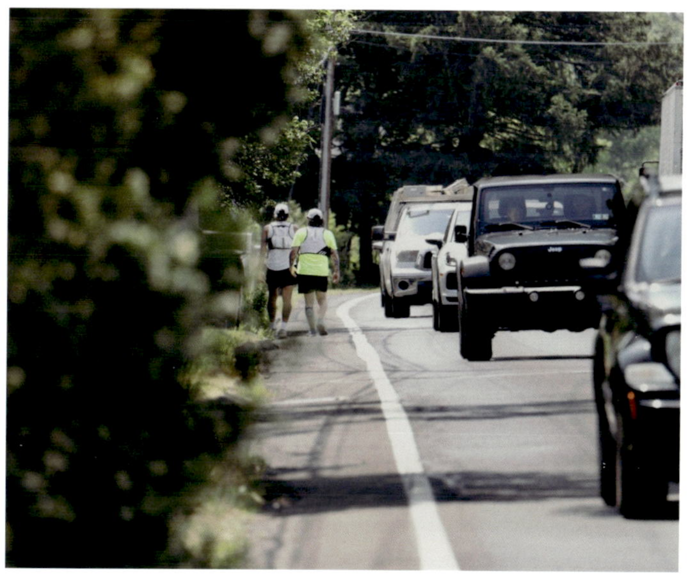

FIG. 10 Nathan Young (right) and Yatika Starr Fields (left) at the start of the Walking Purchase, Wrightstown Friends Meeting, Wrightstown, Pennsylvania, 2023. Photo by Jen McHugh

FIG. 11 Nathan Young (right) and Yatika Starr Fields (left) walking the Walking Purchase route, Pineville, Pennsylvania, 2023. Photo by Jen McHugh

Wrightstown Friends Meeting. By reversing a portion of the path, the artist subverts the act of violence inflicted upon the Lenape and reasserts his inheritance and rights to his ancestral land. Young, known for his innovative multidisciplinary practice, often explores political and spiritual themes in his work. He is a founding member of the artist collective Postcommodity (2007–2015). Below, Young speaks of his family and the work he created for this exhibition, *Alëmi pëmëske* (*He begins to walk*) (Plate 37).

> My experience as a Delaware/Lenape is deeply tied to my family name. I come from the Young family on my father's side and I am also from the Chapman (Pawnee Nation) and Kauley (Kiowa Tribe) families on my mother's side. My knowledge of our Delaware family history begins with my fifth great-grandfather, John Young, for whom my younger brother is named. My name, Nathan "Buck" Young IV, comes from Grandfather John's son, my fourth great-grandfather, Nathan Young. I also have the great fortune of having been given my Unami Lenape name by Nora Dean Thompson during a Native American Church ceremony.
>
> My name is Sukpèkinùnt, which means "He Who Appears Like a Waterfall." The legacy of John Young looms large over my small Delaware family. It is my understanding that John led a notable life. As one document describes, "There is no phase of the development of this section of the country with which John Young is not familiar and those events which are to others historical chronicles are to him matters of personal knowledge or experience." The article goes on to state that "John had the honor of meeting Presidents Roosevelt and Taft and has made four trips to Washington, DC, while he has also visited New York City."
>
> John, an orphan in the tribe, was raised by the notable Delaware leader John Journeycake and was named John because they called him young John, which the Indian agent found convenient and therefore legally recorded his name as John Young. Like the rest of his tribe, John was forced to move from Lawrence, Kansas, to the northeastern part of Indian Territory, near what is today Copan, Oklahoma. John became a leader among the Delaware. Eventually, the district and a lake in the area were named in his honor. It was there that John married Miss Ella Thomas and established a ranch and farm. Soon thereafter his son, Nathan Young, began to operate the ranch. Nathan also worked in the oil fields for the Trinity Oil Drillers Company. He married Miss Irene Brookshire, who had three children, including their first son Nathan (Junior), who we called Grandpa Young.
>
> My Grandpa Young married Miss Betty Warwick in Dewey, Oklahoma, and after serving in World War II he worked for Phillips Petroleum pumping gas as a young man and eventually becoming a Director of Engineering Services for the company before his retirement after fifty years. During his time at Phillips, my grandfather Nathan worked for, and was friends with, two notable Native Americans. The first was W. W. Keeler, president and chairman of the board of Phillips, who in 1974 became the first elected leader of the modern Cherokee Nation. My Grandfather Nathan also worked for and was friends with a fellow Delaware, Leo Johnstone, the vice-chairman of the board of directors of Phillips, who my Grandfather Nathan also worked with on the Delaware Tribal Business Committee for many years; today, this is what we call the Delaware Tribal Council. My father, Nathan's eldest son, Nathan H. Young III, became an attorney and expert in federal tribal law, working for many of the tribes in Oklahoma during his career. Today, my younger brother, John Young, carries on this tradition as an attorney and tribal law specialist. As for myself, I have had the great fortune of becoming an artist. I have heard the saying "to name is to direct." And I am of the belief that my name and my brother's name, Nathan and John, are the reasons we remain so tightly bound to our Delaware/Lenape ancestors, tribe, and family history.
>
> To my knowledge, all of us have continued in the tradition of our Great-Grandfather John as a servant-leader of the Delaware Tribe in some capacity. My Grandfather Young, Aunt Wathene Young, my father, and myself have served as elected leaders on the Delaware Tribal Council and, in the case of my brother and

father, judges on the Delaware Court. I believe our family values of servant leadership to our tribe were engrained in us by the legacy and life that John Young lived when the Delaware/Lenape were forced to Indian Territory from Kansas, leaving his descendants, his family, with a clear path to follow.

My family experience as a Delaware/Lenape has deeply informed my art practice. My long-form video work, re-creating what is possible of the notorious Walking Purchase, reflects this idea. The video *Alëmi pëmëske* (*He begins to walk*) is a feeble attempt at re-creating an event that my ancestors lived and that became a major chapter of the myth-making of the United States: how lands were first stolen from the original Nations of this continent.

I cannot know this experience, and my artwork is only a representation of how I wish to express a story that I am sure the Delaware/Lenape do not want to be remembered for. We are not victims; we are now many nations, bodies made of families and communities who have stayed together for hundreds of years after exile from Lenapehoking. The Delaware/Lenape were made to walk from their homes countless times in our history since contact. I would like my artwork to be understood as a process of trying to understand, attempting to grapple with something that no person should ever experience but has become well known as a part of our history.

Contemporary Delaware/Lenape cannot know that feeling. Nor should they. I chose to become an artist to freely engage ideas, and my experience as an American Indian is rich with complexities to attempt to understand. *Alëmi pëmëske* (*He begins to walk*) is a long-form video art piece that for me expresses the futility of truly understanding history by re-creating something that is impossible to understand. I choose to focus on the landscape because I do not believe a cinematic recreation of the event could honestly depict the hardships and violence my ancestors endured. I can only bring attention to change, and in this art piece there is an imaginary landscape that haunts this walk. It haunts because it is the specter of guilt that exists in the underlying knowledge that this land, what you are seeing, still holds the pain of those past transgressions, whether one thinks of the Lenape or history at all.

One could not think of the Lenape and not still feel this pain. It lasts in the damage to the environment, it lasts in the economic disparities of those who currently call Lenapchoking home, and it lasts in the collective memory of my community. We will always know Lenapehoking is our homeland, no matter where we may call home today.[8]

Jim Rementer

It is appropriate to recognize here the contributions of Jim Rementer, the Delaware Tribe of Indian's language keeper, who has assisted with the Lenape language included in this exhibition.

His story originates in Philadelphia where he grew up as a descendant of the white settlers who arrived in the eighteenth century in what is now Pennsylvania. Told in third person below, his story speaks to the desire to make tangible the obscured history and language of the Lenape.

> Jim Rementer grew up in Ambler, Pennsylvania, a suburb of Philadelphia. His interest in Lenape culture began as a young boy, around the age of six or seven years, when his parents sent him off to summer camp named Camp Lenape, located in Fairview Lake, Pennsylvania. There he met his first true "Indians," two counselors who were Cherokee. Always curious about the Lenape place names he frequently encountered in the area, as a young man he began conducting research at the American Philosophical Society in Philadelphia.
>
> There he came across a series of letters exchanged between Frank Speck and a Lenape named Freddie Washington who lived in Oklahoma, northeast of Copan. Driven by curiosity, Rementer sent a letter to the address listed in the correspondence and it was soon met with a reply. A back-and-forth exchange between Rementer and Washington began immediately. A fascinating story of Lenape life in Oklahoma described by Washington eventually led to an invitation for Rementer

to come out and see for himself. This was the summer of 1961.

Little did Rementer realize, when he boarded the bus for Oklahoma, that his life was about to change forever. When the bus pulled into the bus stop at the intersection of Highway 75 and Main Street, in Dewey, Oklahoma, he off-boarded, only to run right into my uncle John Whiteturkey Fugate. Fugate told him Freddie's house was at least fifteen miles outside of town, and there was no public transportation. He suggested Rementer head over to the Phillips 66 service station and ask about hitching a ride north to Freddie's place.

Eventually, Rementer got a ride and he arrived at Washington's place in the early evening. Exhausted from the thirty-seven-hour bus ride, he wanted nothing more than to go to bed, but then Frederick Falleaf appeared at the front door, announcing there was a Stomp Dance that night at the Falleaf allotment and Jim was invited. Jim returned from the dance grounds at about 3 a.m. This hectic pace was common during the month that he stayed with the Washingtons and made notes on the Lenape language in journals.

During this period, he met several fluent Lenape speakers, each with stories of the tribe's removal from their ancestral land, and each with concerns that the language might be lost. Nora Thompson Dean was one of the speakers Jim interviewed. When he returned to Oklahoma the following summer in 1962, Dean suggested he stay with her family instead of taking an apartment. Generosity is one of the Lenape virtues, and such acts by the Dean family demonstrate an ancient practice of the Lenape people: "We are all relatives, stressing the interconnectivity of all things. Indeed, the land, sky, and all of life exists as an interdependent, interconnected web, where no single element or being is void of its own place and embodied spirit."[9] Rementer's arrangement with Dean lasted for sixty years, as Rementer never returned to his native Pennsylvania but stayed in Oklahoma meticulously recording and journaling the Lenape language. His efforts at this critical time in the history of the tribe resulted in the Lenape Talking Dictionary, a vibrant resource of Lenape language, stories, and history that is still in use today.[10]

Elànkumàk (my relatives) are a foundational theme in the work of the contemporary artists in this exhibition, each of whom has unique ties to Lenape land as a descendant. This fact seems particularly significant as there has never before been an exhibition of contemporary Lenape artists in Pennsylvania who can trace their families back to the time of the Walking Purchase and William Penn. As survivors of colonial practices that erase Indigenous histories, cultures, and expressions, they assert their inheritance of succession and the art they create. Family is essential to an understanding of one's place in the world. The artists in this exhibition grew up on the "edges of two very distinct cultures, western European and American Indian."[11] They are the expression of both Western European education and the education they received from their American Indian families and communities. They create in the space between the expected and the unexpected. *Lankuntuwakan* (relationship, peace, and a deeper understanding of well-being) is where creativity is an interconnected web to both past and present and can heal the historical traumas of separation from home and the erasure of presence.

> Life, you know, is like light. It is continuous. It is our eyes that seek beginnings and endings. I was trying to find an ending with my pencil, but all I found was that there was no ending.
>
> —Walter Anderson[12]

Notes

1 Gerald Vizenor, ed., *Survivance: Narratives of Native Presence* (Lincoln: University of Nebraska Press, 2008).

2 Sarah B. Shear, Ryan T. Knowles, Gregory J. Soden, and Antonio J. Castro, "Manifesting Destiny: Re/presentations of Indigenous Peoples in K-12 U.S. History Standards," *Theory & Research in Social Education* 43, no. 1 (2015): 68-101; Dr. Rachel Talbert, email to author, May 15, 2023.

3 "An heir is a person who is legally entitled to collect an inheritance when a deceased person did not formalize a last will and testament." Julian Kagan, "What is an Heir? Definition, Dying Intestate, and Examples," Investopedia, published September 21, 2022, https://www.investopedia.com/terms/h/heir.asp.

4 Ahchipaptunhe (David L. Haff), email to author, May 2, 2023.

5 Holly Wilson, "Bloodline," accessed May 30, 2023, https://hollywilson.com/portfolio/bloodline/.

6 Joe Baker, "Native Identity in an Age of Hybridity," in *Remix: New Modernities in a Post-Indian World*, ed. Joe Baker and Gerald McMaster (Washington, DC: National Museum of the American Indian, 2007), 25.

7 See essays by Laura Turner Igoe and Joel Whitney in this volume.

8 Nathan Young, email to author, lightly edited, May 30, 2023.

9 Joe Baker, Hadrien Coumans, and Chelsea Kimura, "Myth of the Purchase of Manhattan," in *Lenapehoking: An Anthology*, ed. Joe Baker, Hadrien Coumans, and Joel Whitney (New York: The Lenape Center and Brooklyn Public Library, 2022), 26.

10 Jim Rementer, interview by author, May 28, 2023. For the Lenape Talking Dictionary, see https://www.talk-lenape.org/.

11 Vine Deloria, Jr., *Red Earth, White Lies: Native Americans and the Myth of Scientific Fact* (New York: Scribner, 1997), xiii.

12 Christopher Maurer, *Fortune's Favorite Child: The Uneasy Life of Walter Anderson* (Jackson: University Press of Mississippi, 2003), 290.

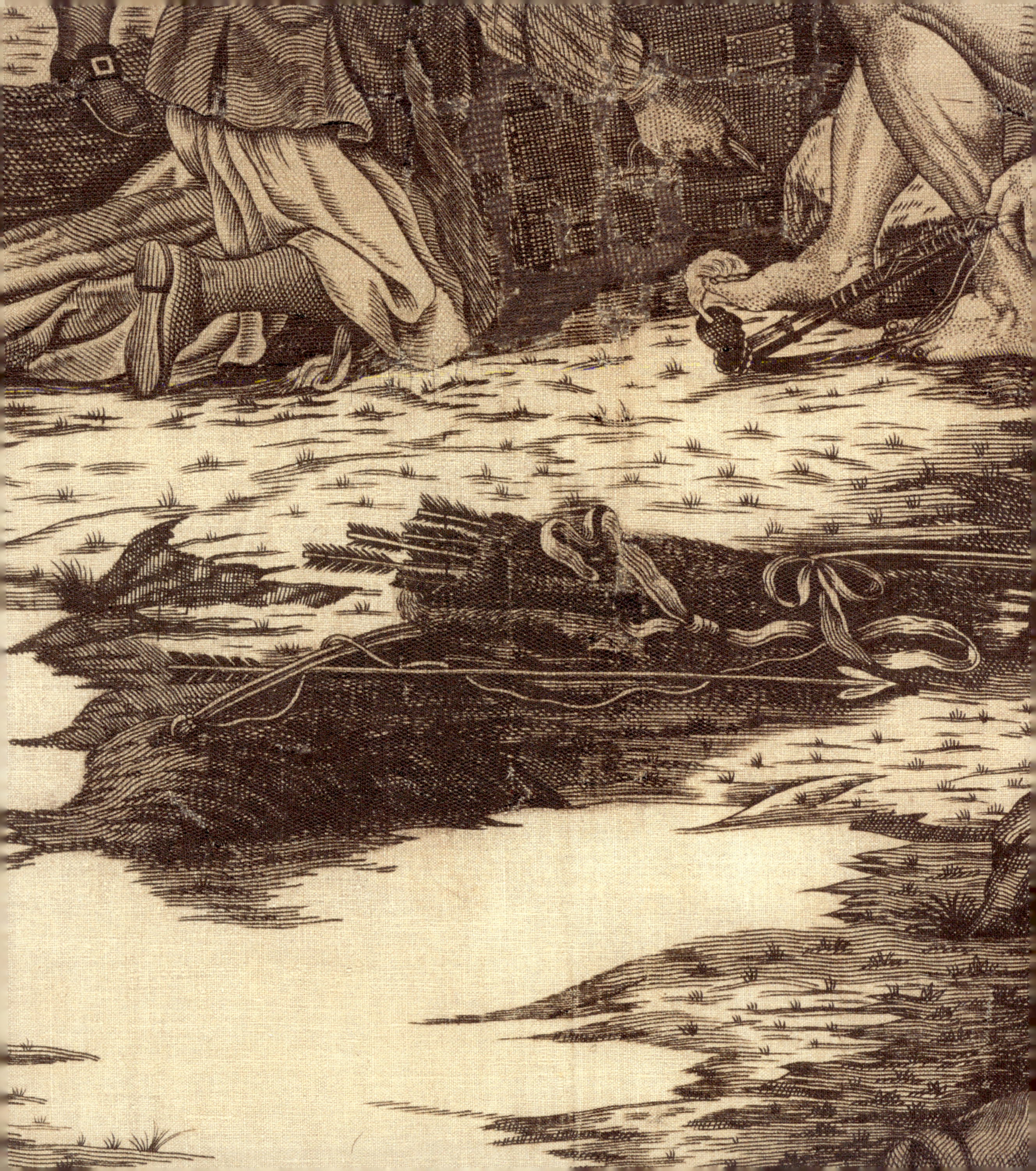

Plates

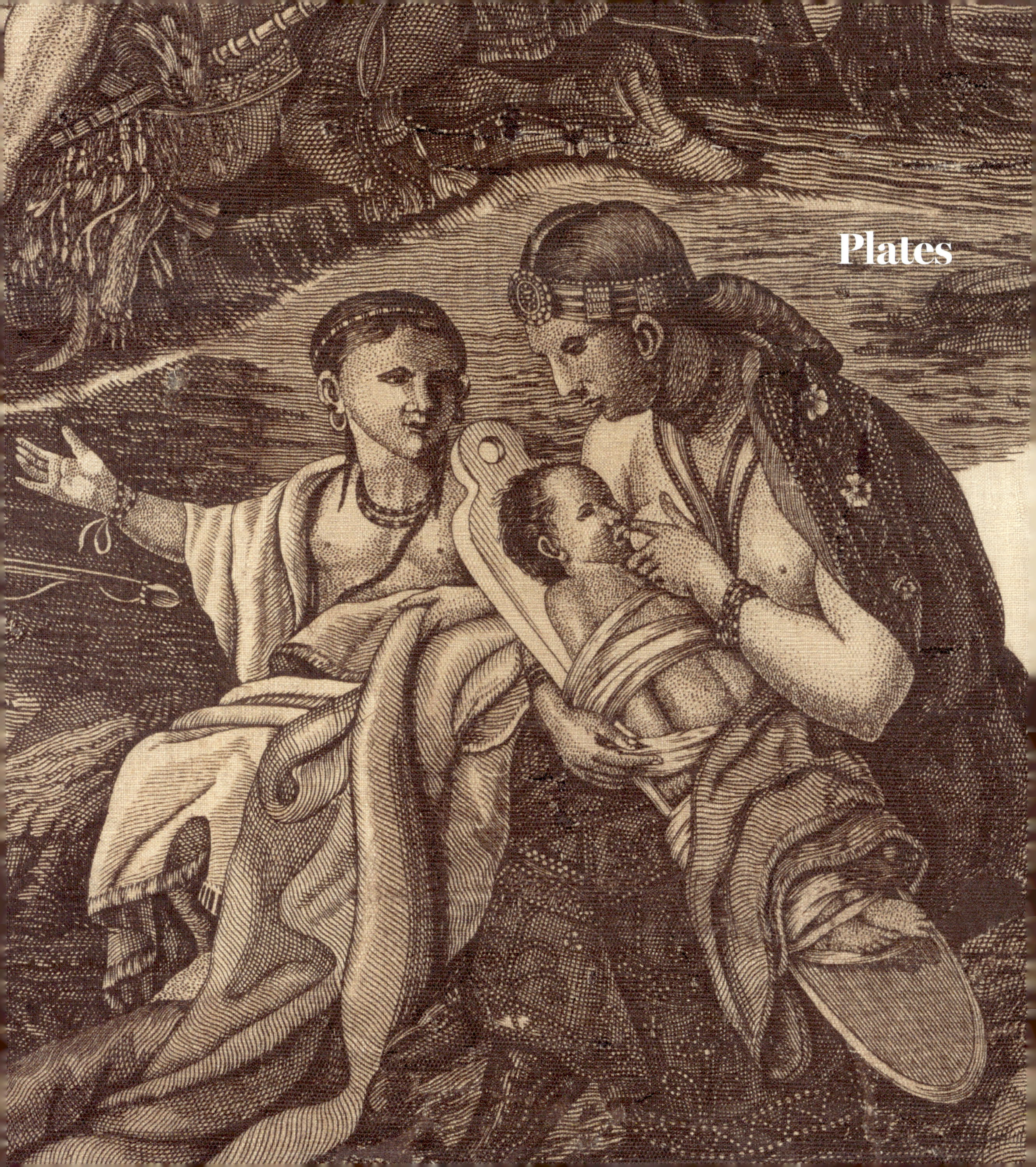

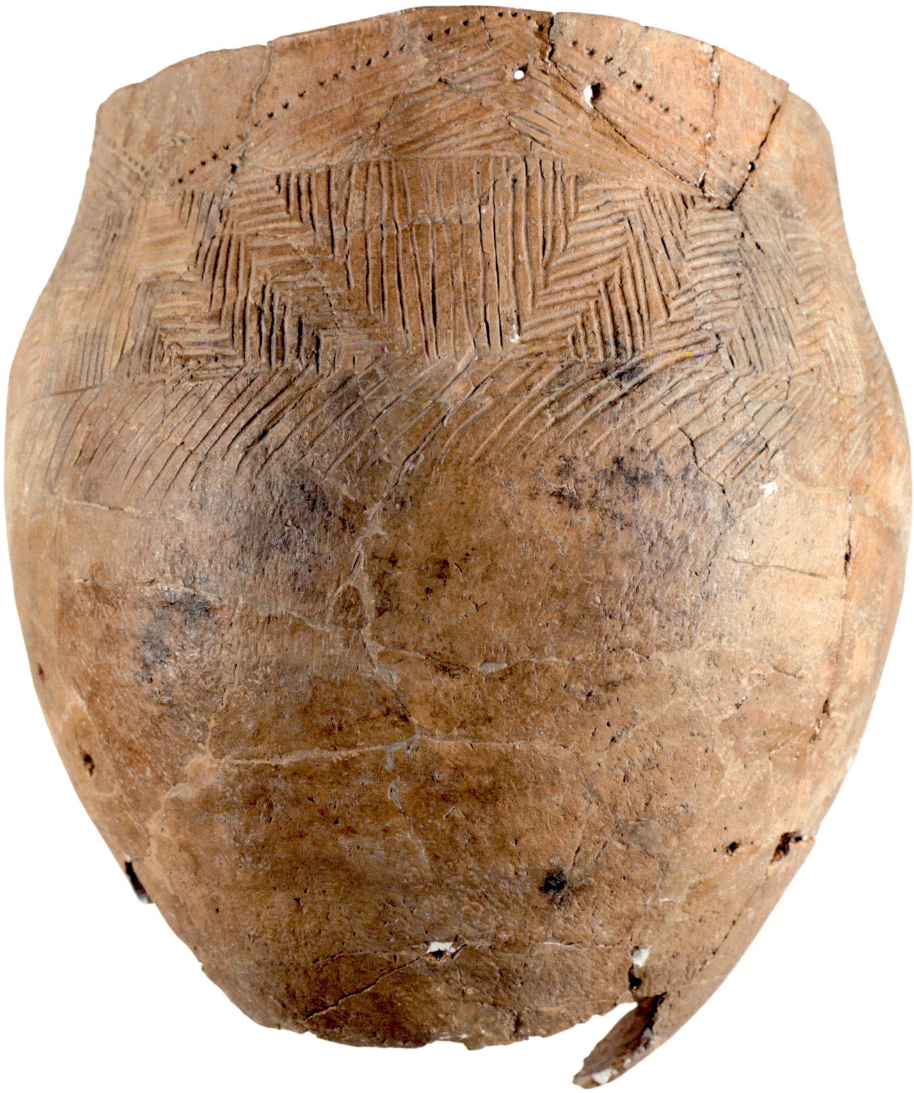

PLATE 1

Artist Unknown

Cooking Vessel, Signal Hill, Late Woodland Period (1000–1350 CE)

Ceramic, 13 × 9½ × 9½ inches. Courtesy of the New Jersey State Museum

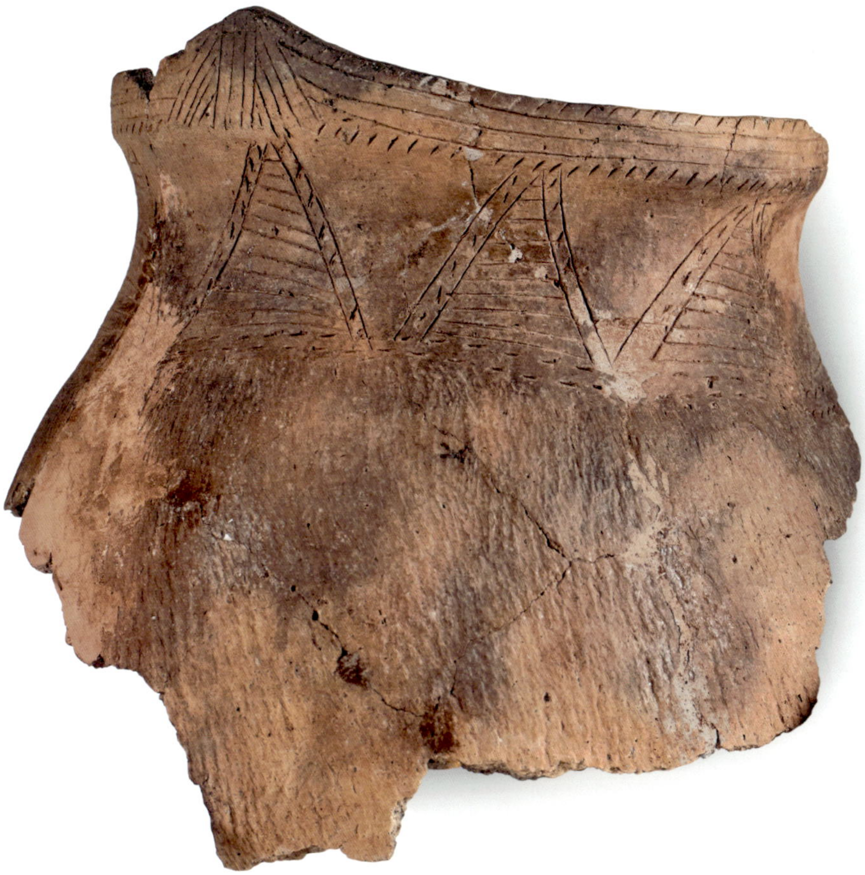

PLATE 2

Artist Unknown

Minisink Jar Fragment, Late Woodland Period (1250–1400 CE)

Ceramic, 9 × 8¼ × 8¼ inches. Courtesy of the New Jersey State Museum, Charles A. Philhower Collection, 1970

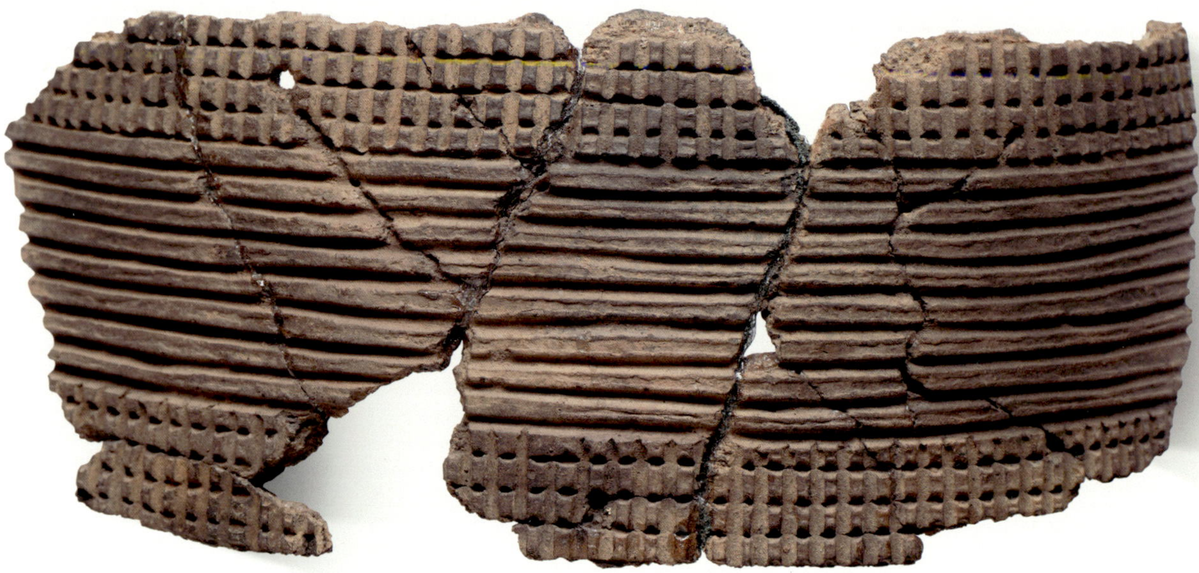

PLATE 3

Artist Unknown

Incised Vessel Fragment, Late Woodland Period (1000–1600 CE)

Ceramic, 4½ × 11½ × ½ inches. Courtesy of the New Jersey State Museum, Abbott Farm Collection, 1936

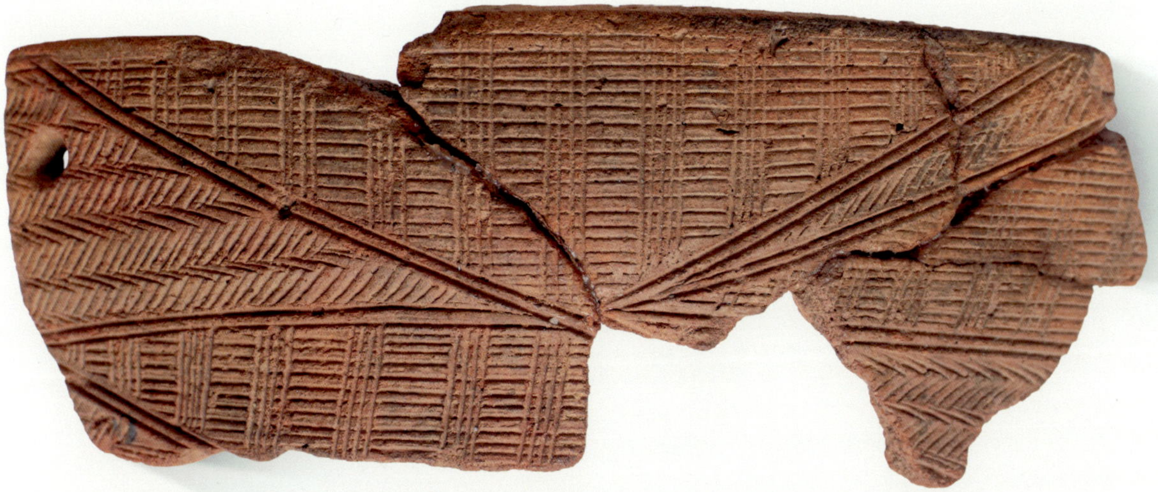

PLATE 4

Artist Unknown

Abbott Zoned Vessel Fragment, Middle Woodland Period (200–800 CE)

Ceramic, 6¾ × 4¾ × ½ inches. Courtesy of the New Jersey State Museum, Abbott Farm Collection, 1936

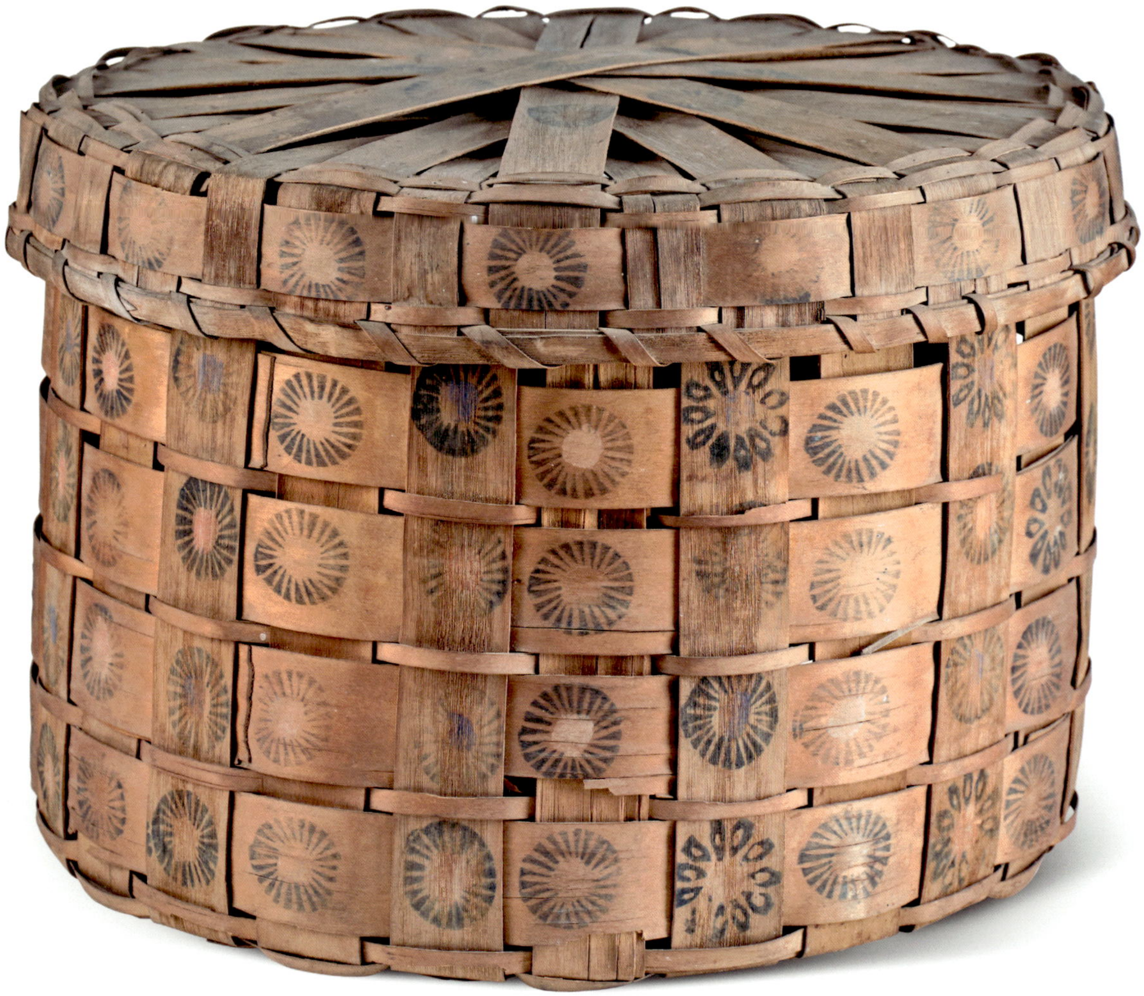

PLATE 5

Artist Unknown

Stamped Basket, 1880–
early 20th century

Splint wood and dye, 10¼ × 15¼ × 15¼ inches. Courtesy of the New Jersey State Museum, Charles A. Philhower Collection, 1970

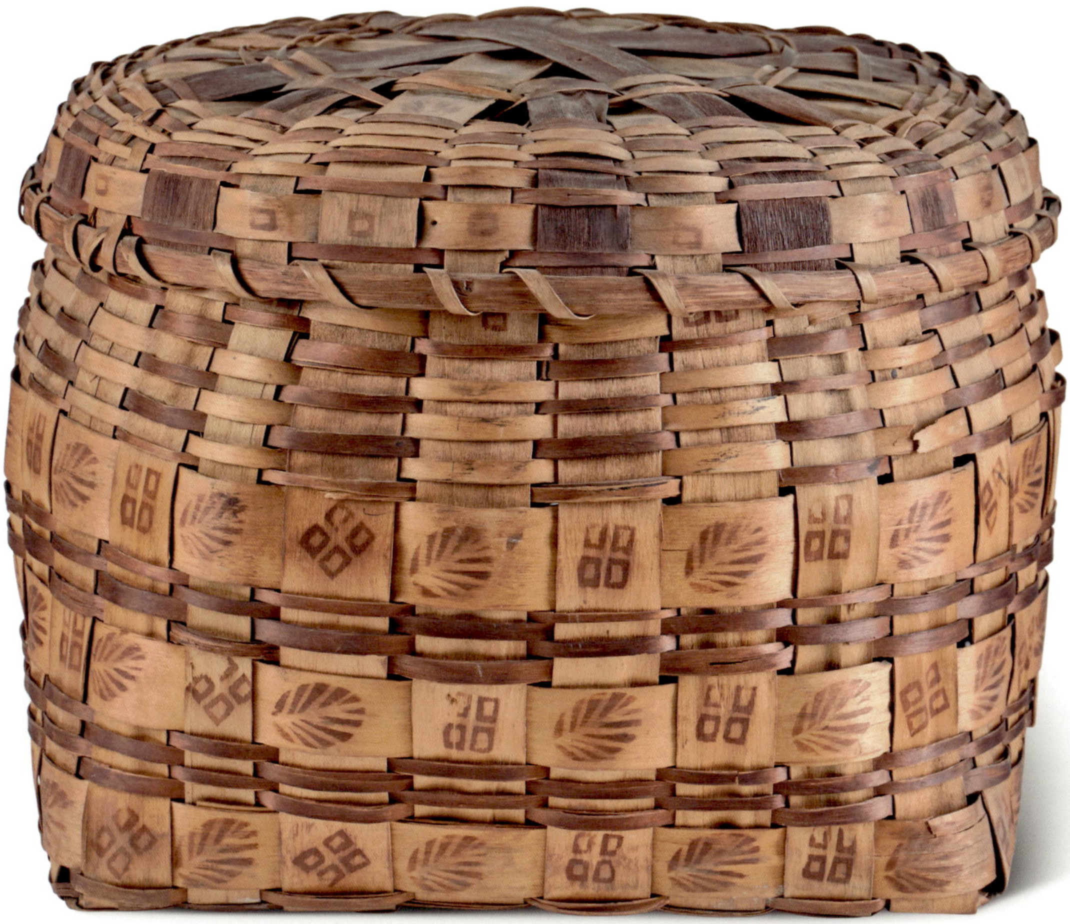

PLATE 6

Artist Unknown

Stamped Basket, 1880–
early 20th century

Splint wood and dye, 10½ × 15 × 15 inches. Courtesy of the New Jersey State Museum, Charles A. Philhower Collection, 1970

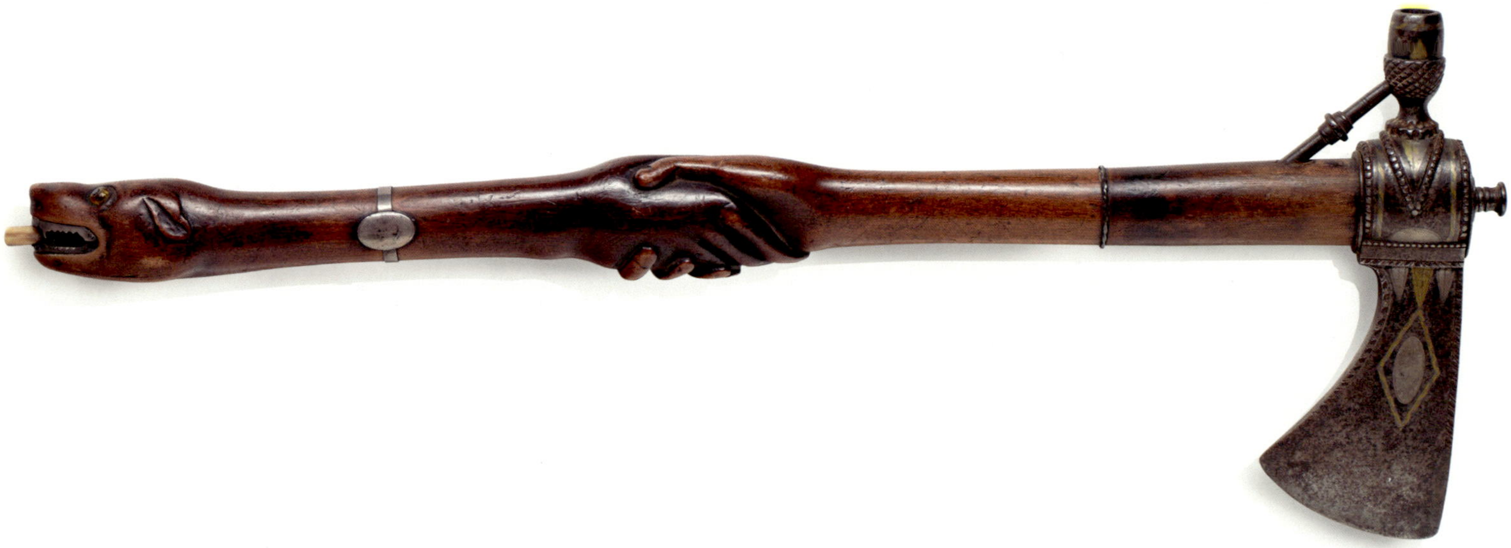

PLATE 7

Artist Unknown (British)

Pipe Tomahawk, late 18th to early 19th century

Wood, brass, and steel, 2 × 18½ × 7 inches. Courtesy of the New Jersey State Museum, Charles A. Philhower Collection, 1970

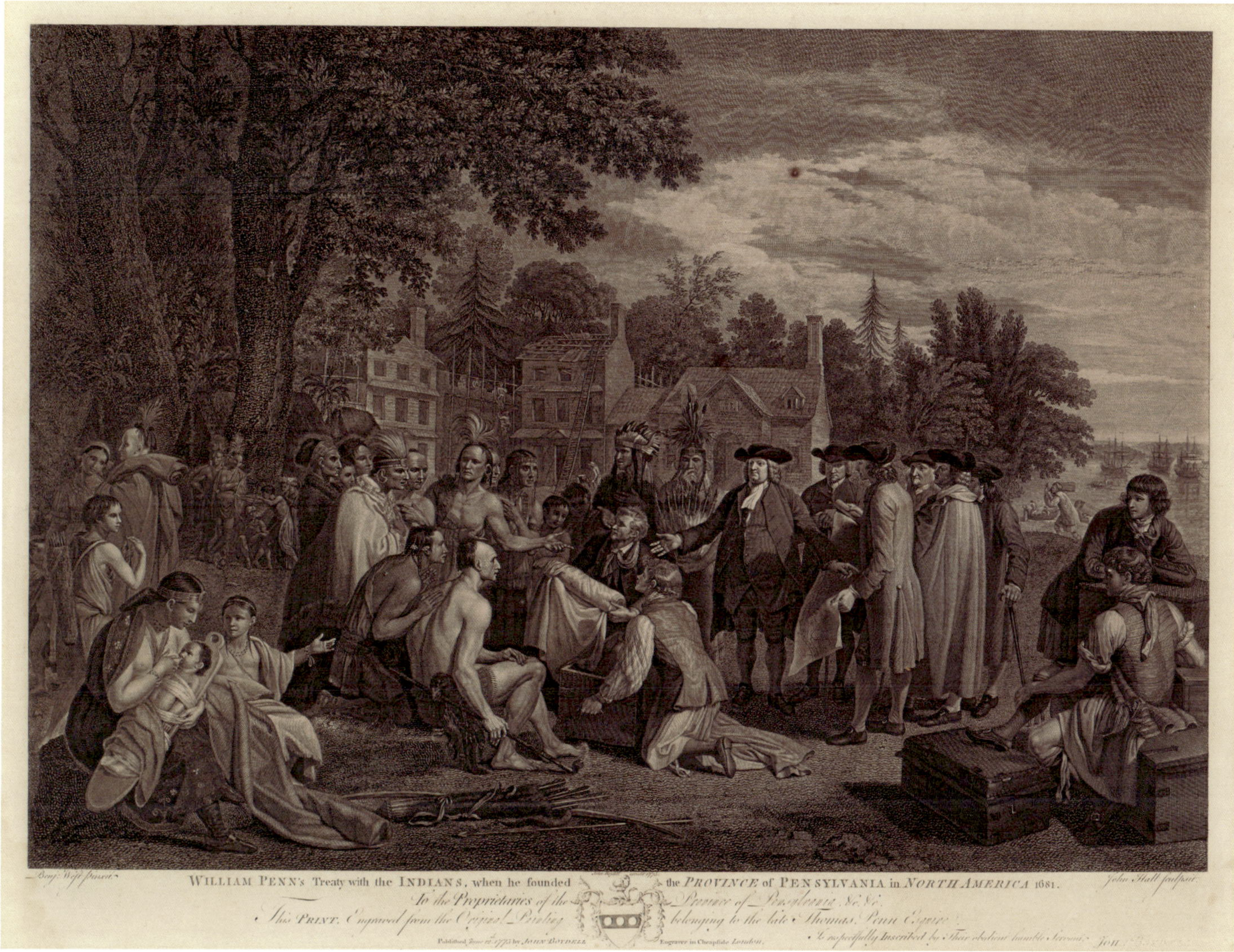

PLATE 8

John Hall (1739–1797),
after Benjamin West

William Penn's Treaty with the Indians, 1775

Engraving, 24 7/16 × 19 1/16 inches. Philadelphia Museum of Art: Gift of Henry Goddard Leach, 1939, 1939-34-1

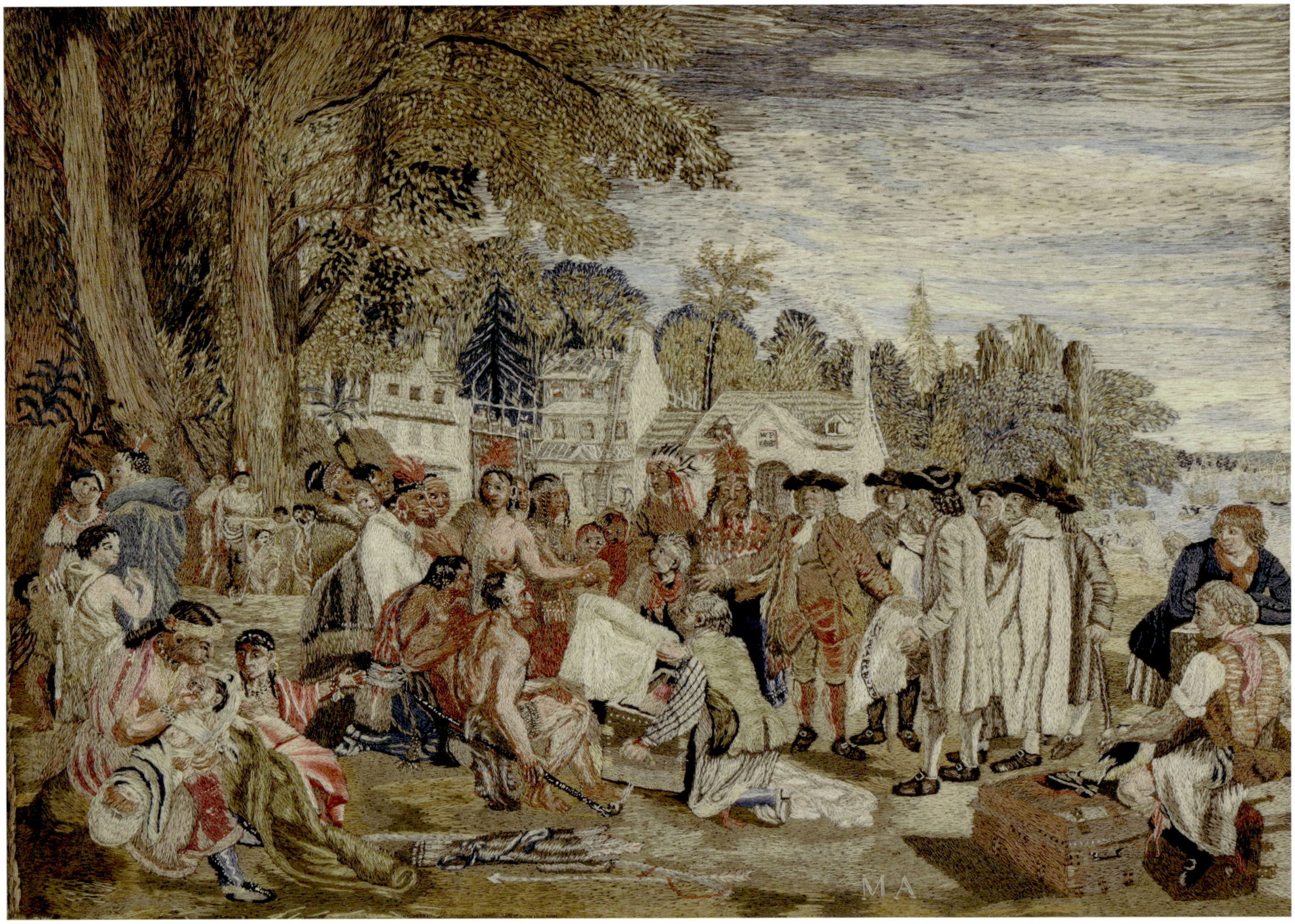

PLATE 9

Margaret Ansell

Penn's Treaty with the Indians,
1771–1776

Wool, linen, and silk, 16¼ × 22¾ inches. Gift of Julie and the late Carl M. Lindberg, Courtesy of Winterthur Museum, Garden & Library

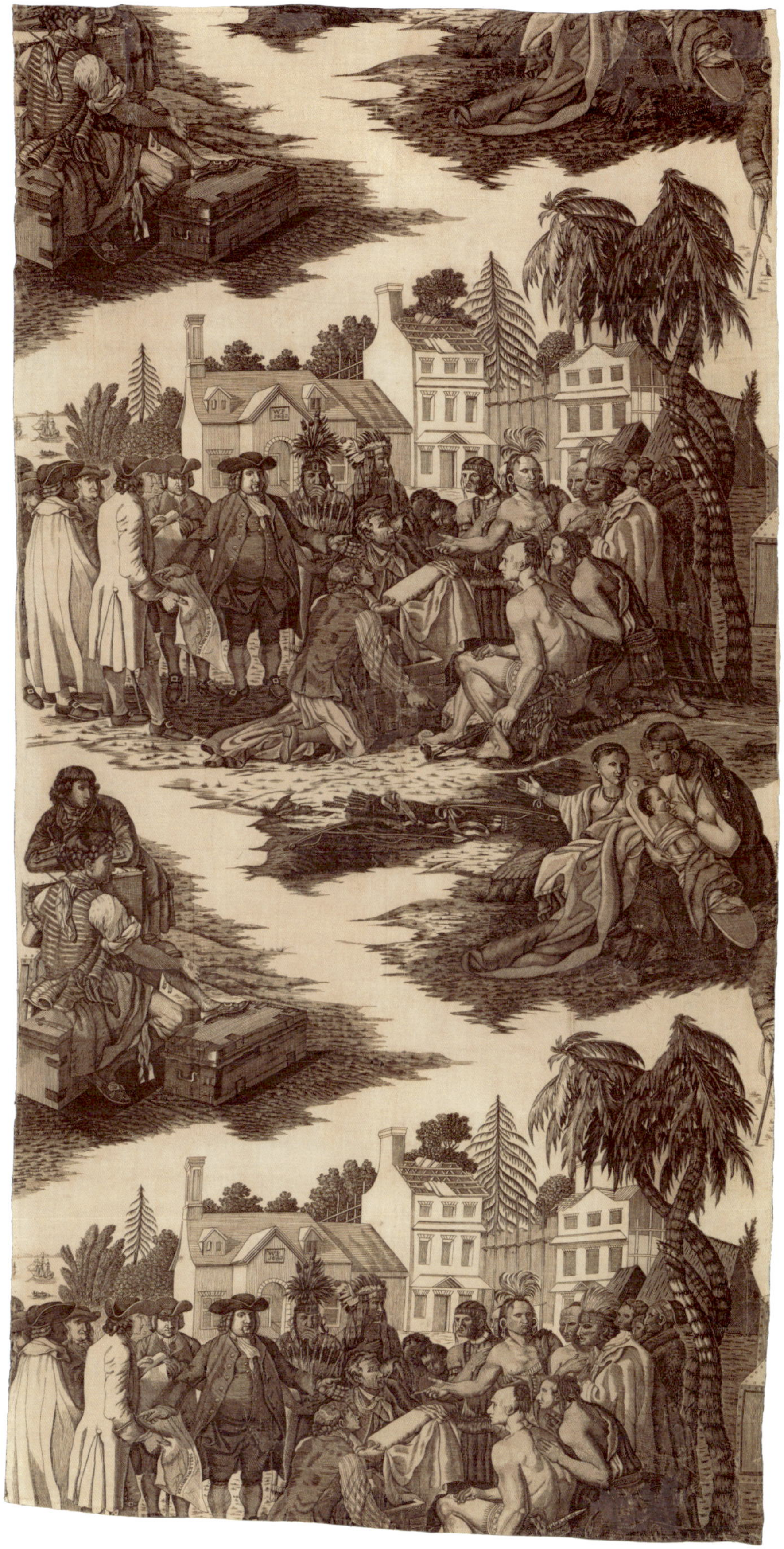

PLATE 10

Artist Unknown (British)

William Penn's Treaty with the Indians, ca. 1785

Copperplate print on cotton, 58½ × 29½ inches. Philadelphia Museum of Art: Purchased with funds contributed by the Women's Committee and the Craft Show Committee of the Philadelphia Museum of Art, 1976, 1976-43-1a,b

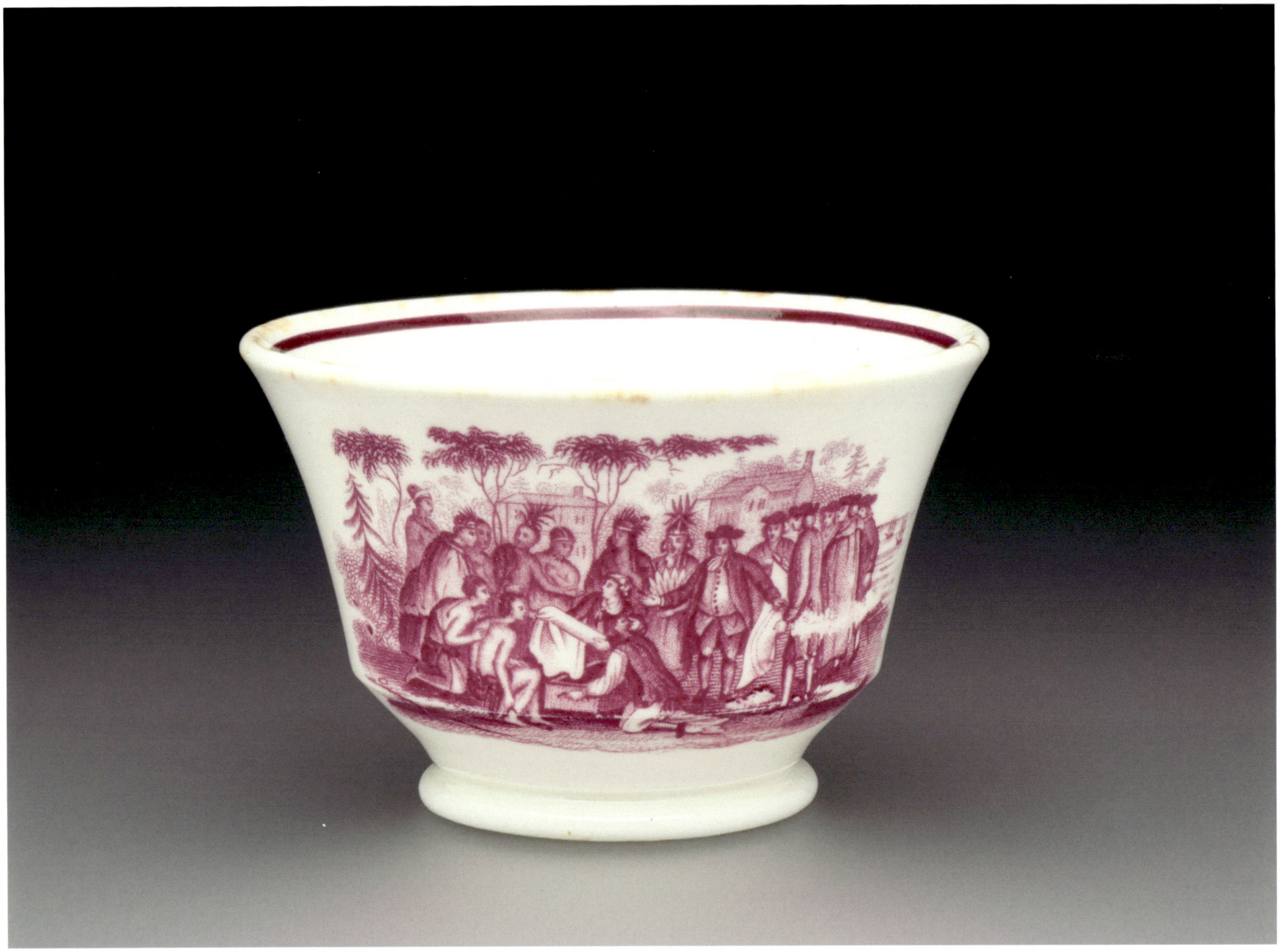

PLATE 11

Artist Unknown (British)

Tea Bowl with William Penn's Treaty with the Indians, 1815–1830

Porcelain and lead glaze, 2⅜ × 3⅝ inches. Bequest of Henry Francis du Pont, courtesy of Winterthur Museum, Garden & Library

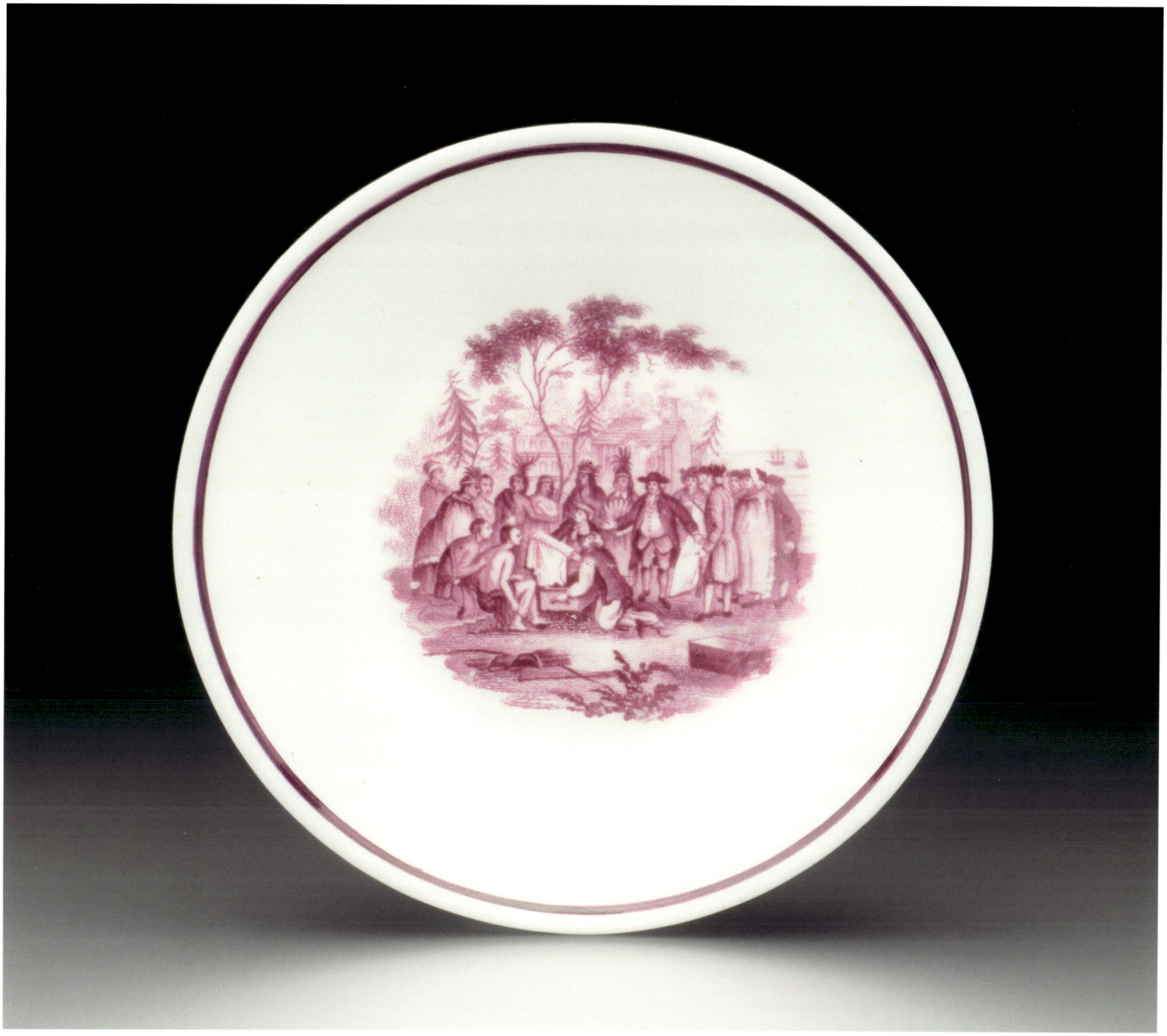

PLATE 12

Artist Unknown (British)

Saucer with William Penn's Treaty with the Indians, 1815–1830

Porcelain and lead glaze, 1¼ × 5½ inches. Bequest of Henry Francis du Pont, courtesy of Winterthur Museum, Garden & Library

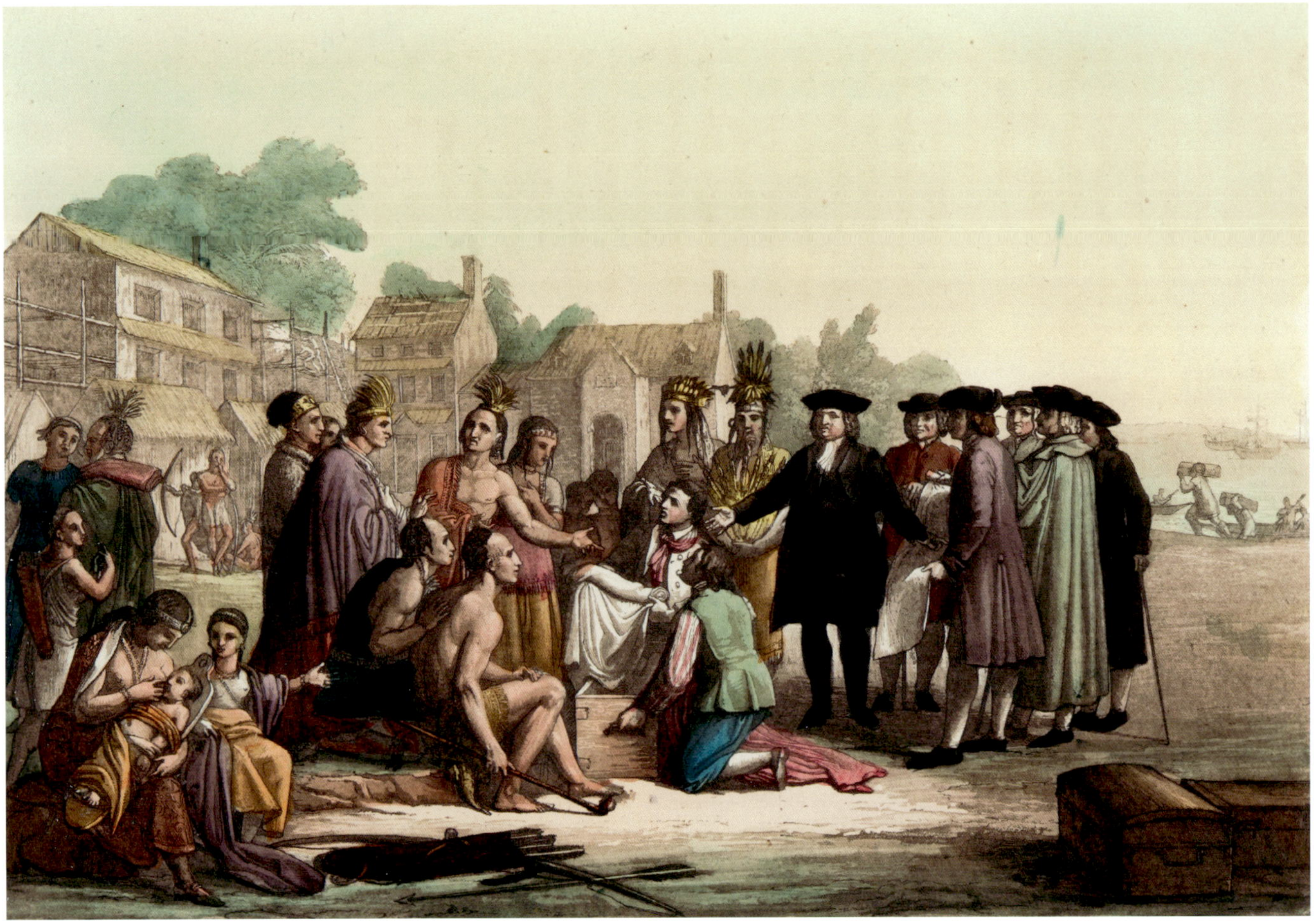

PLATE 13

Gallo Gallina (1796–1874), after Benjamin West

Guillermo Pen echando las primeras bases de la ciudad de Filadelfia

Plate 41 from Giulio Ferrario, *Le Costume Ancien et Moderne* (Milan: G. Ferrario, ca. 1827), Hand-colored aquatint, 6⅞ × 8¾ inches. Philadelphia Museum of Art: Gift of the McNeil Americana Collection, 2012, 2012-172-179

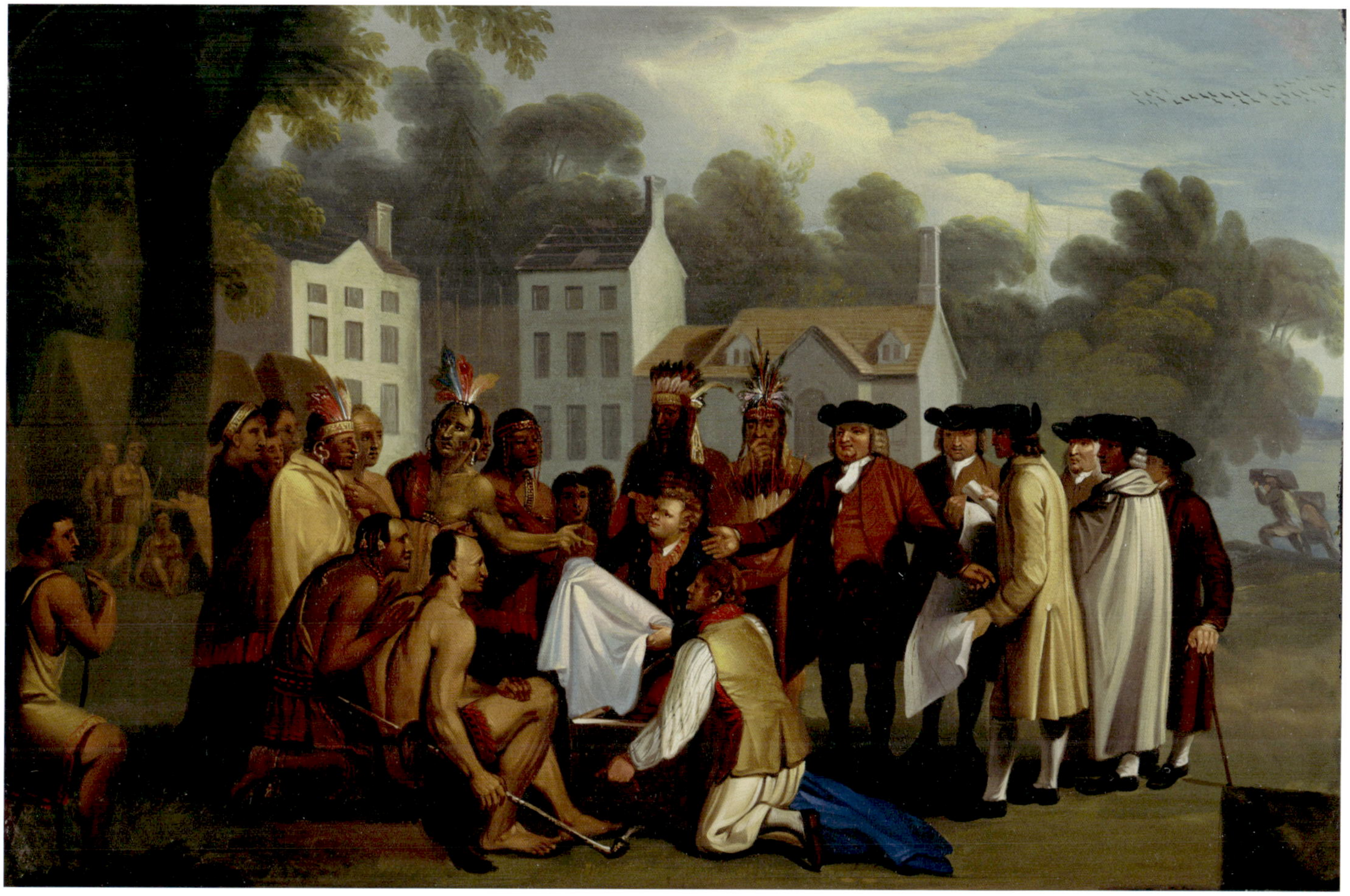

PLATE 14

Artist Unknown (American)

Penn's Treaty with the Indians, 19th century

Oil on ferrous metal, 13½ × 20 inches. Philadelphia Museum of Art: Bequest of Martha Stokes Price, 2014, 2014-40-5

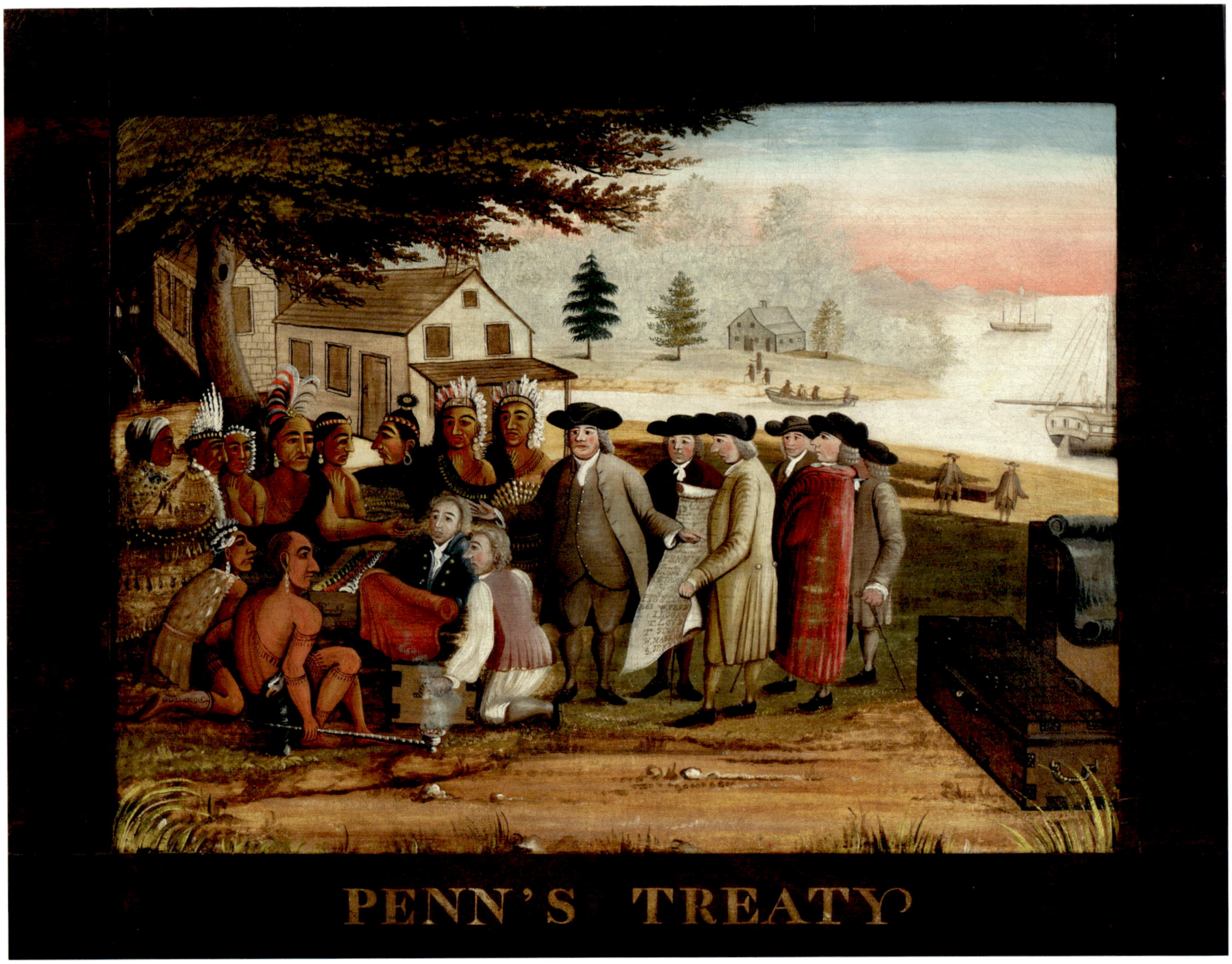

PLATE 15

Edward Hicks (1780–1849)

Penn's Treaty, ca. 1830–1835

Oil on canvas, 17½ × 23½ inches. Philadelphia Museum of Art: 125th Anniversary Acquisition. Gift of the McNeil Americana Collection, 2007, 2007-65-7

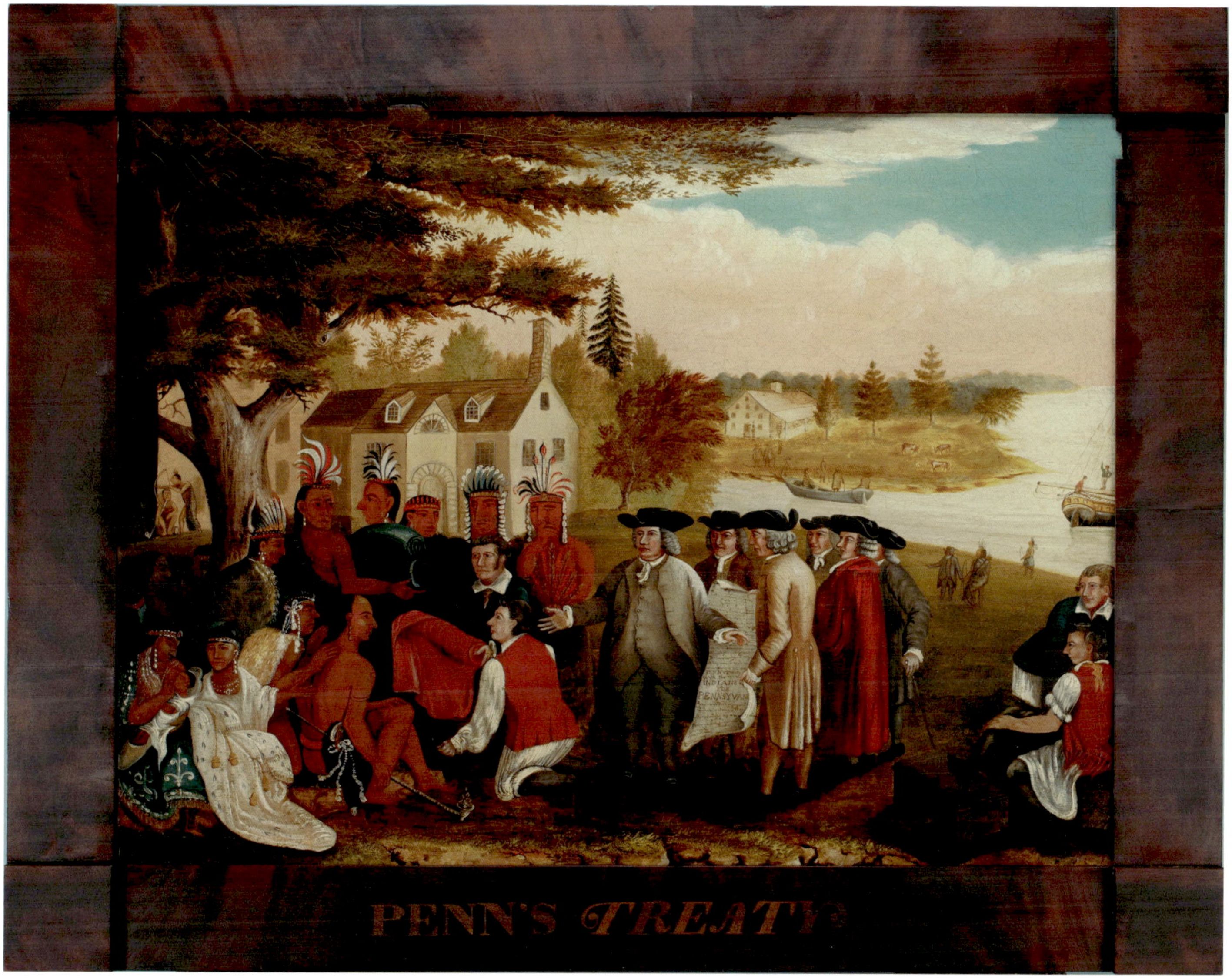

PLATE 16

Edward Hicks (1780–1849)

Penn's Treaty, 1835–1840

Oil on canvas, 20⅞ × 27⅜ inches. Courtesy of the Mercer Museum of the Bucks County Historical Society

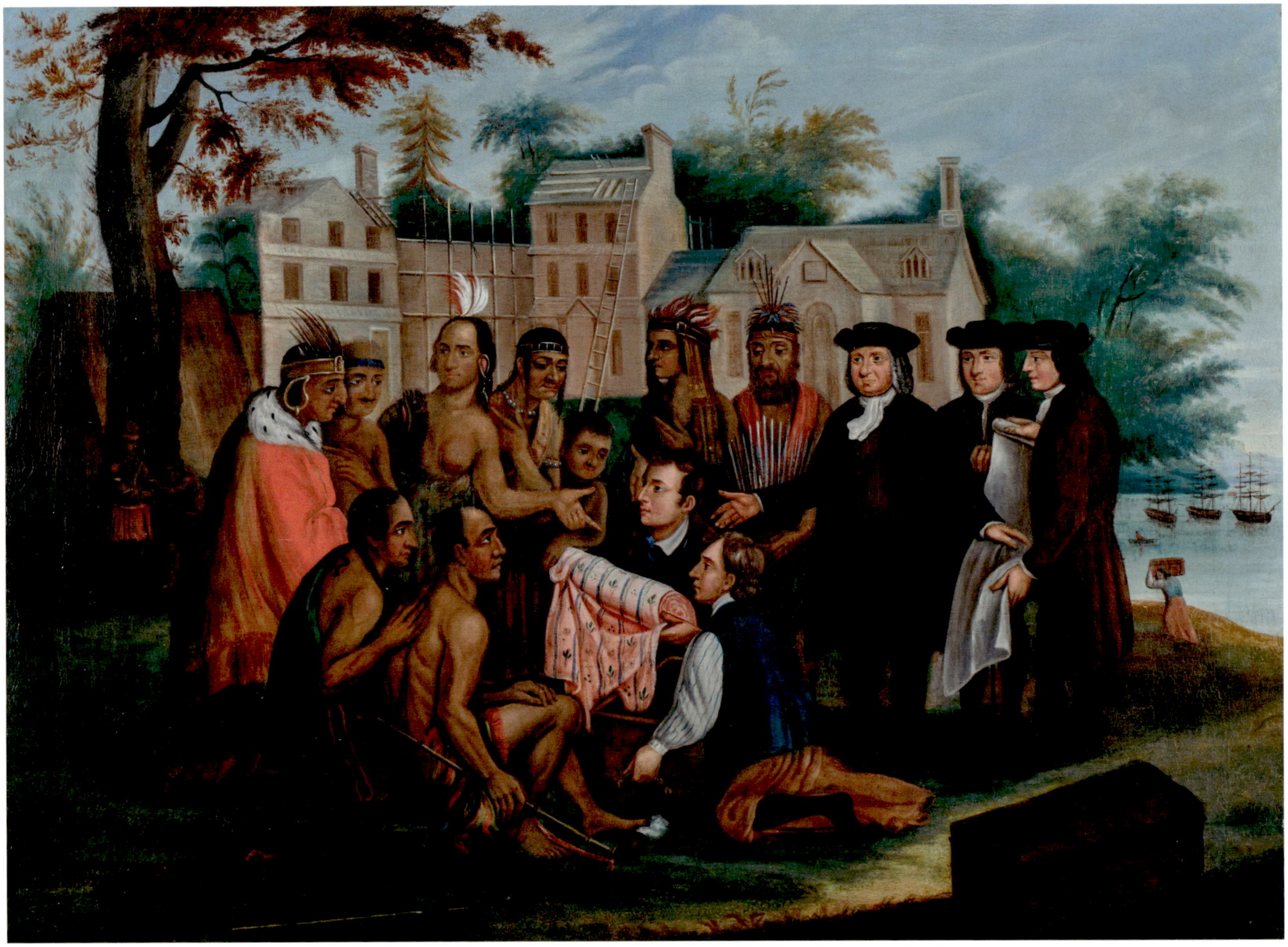

PLATE 17

Edward Hicks (1780–1849)

Penn's Treaty with the Indians, ca. 1840

Oil on canvas, 38 × 48 inches. James A. Michener Art Museum. Gift of Anthony Seraphin in honor of Robert and Joyce Byers, 2022.3.1

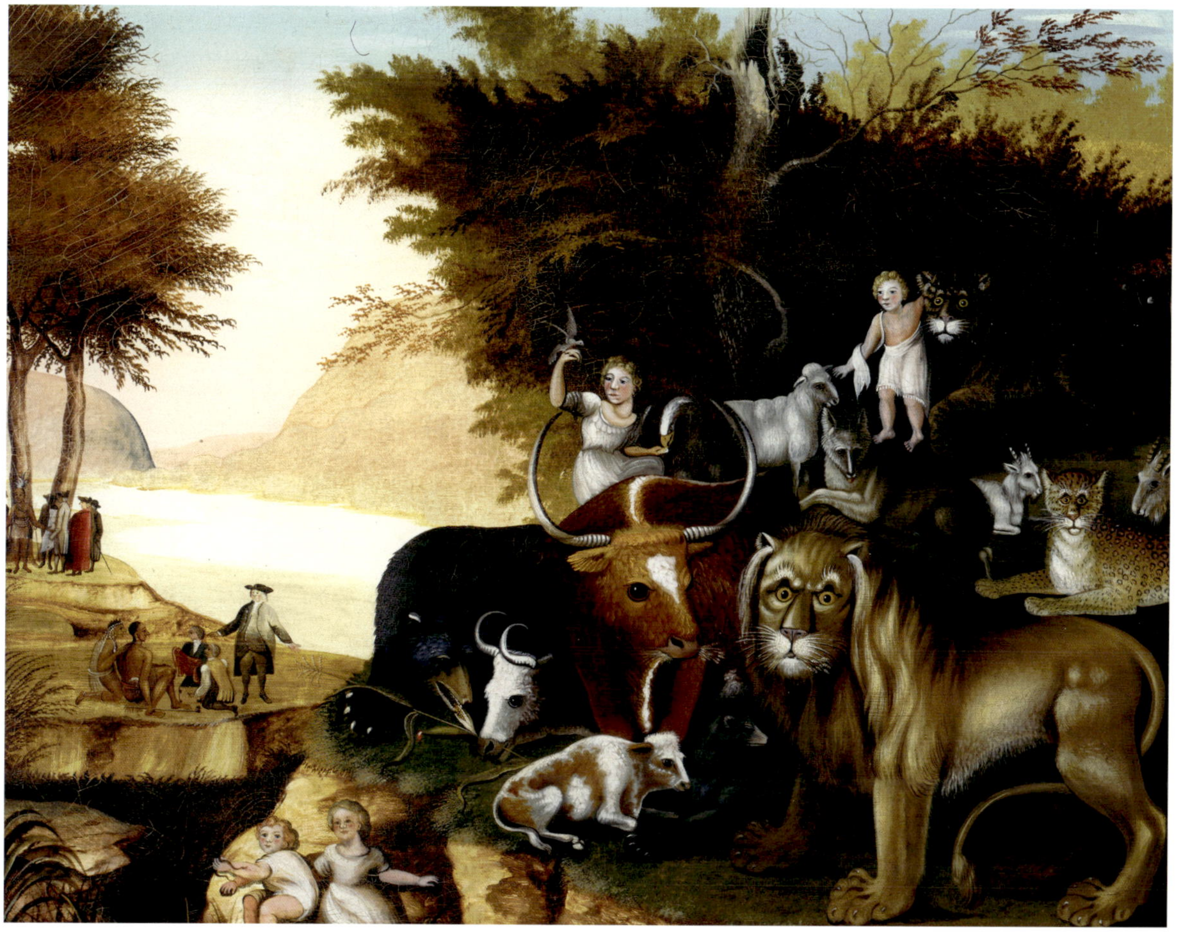

PLATE 18

Edward Hicks (1780–1849)

Peaceable Kingdom, 1835–1837

Oil on canvas, 28 × 35 inches. Courtesy of the Mercer Museum of the Bucks County Historical Society

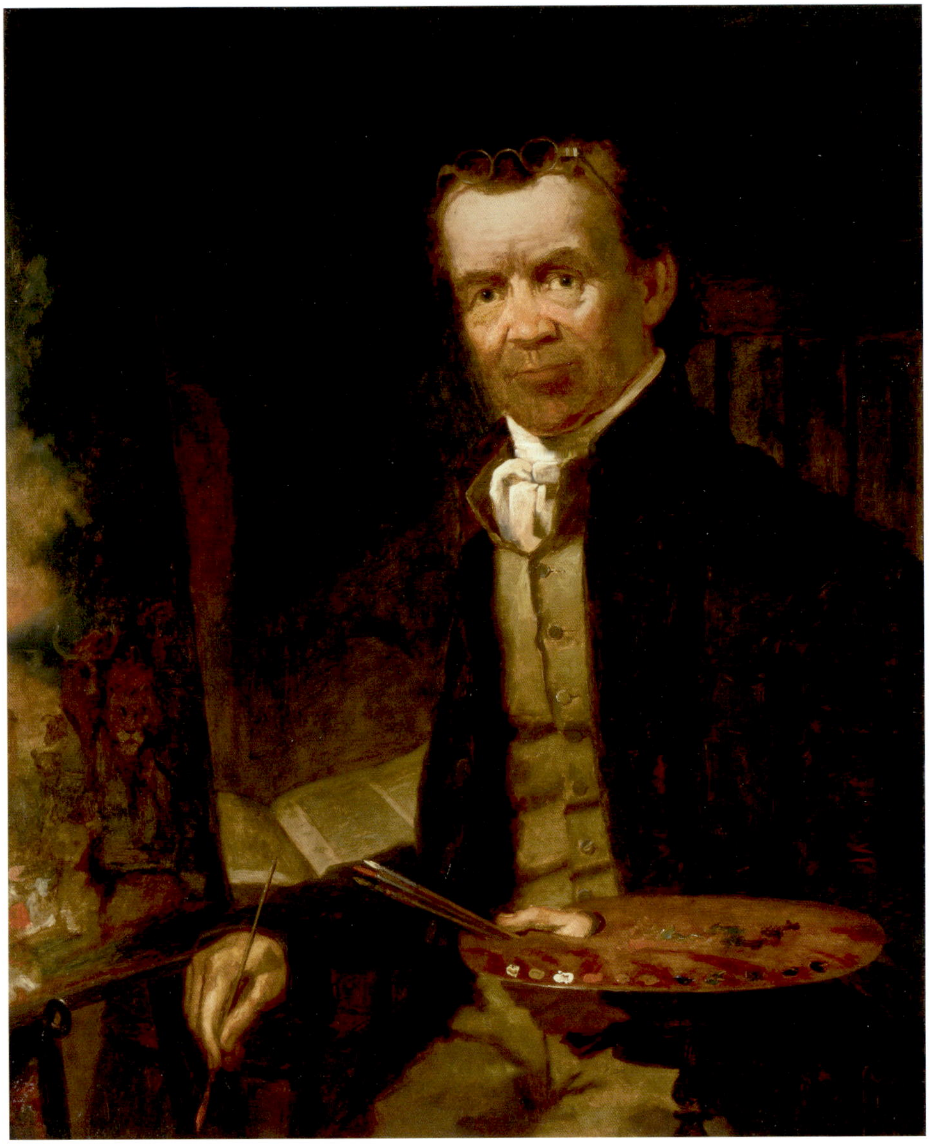

PLATE 19

Thomas Hicks (1823–1890)

Portrait of Edward Hicks, ca. 1850–1852

Oil on canvas, 36⅛ × 29⅛ inches. James A. Michener Art Museum. Museum purchase funded by Eleanor K. Denoon, The Bella S. and Benjamin H. Garb Foundation Inc., Mr. and Mrs. Kenneth Gemmill, George S. Hobensack, Jr., Laurence D. Keller, William Mandel, Members of Newtown Friends Meeting, Olde Hope Antiques, Inc., Residents of Pennswood Village, Eleanor and Malcolm Polis, Ms. Leslie E. Skilton, Kingdon Swayne and Anonymous Donors

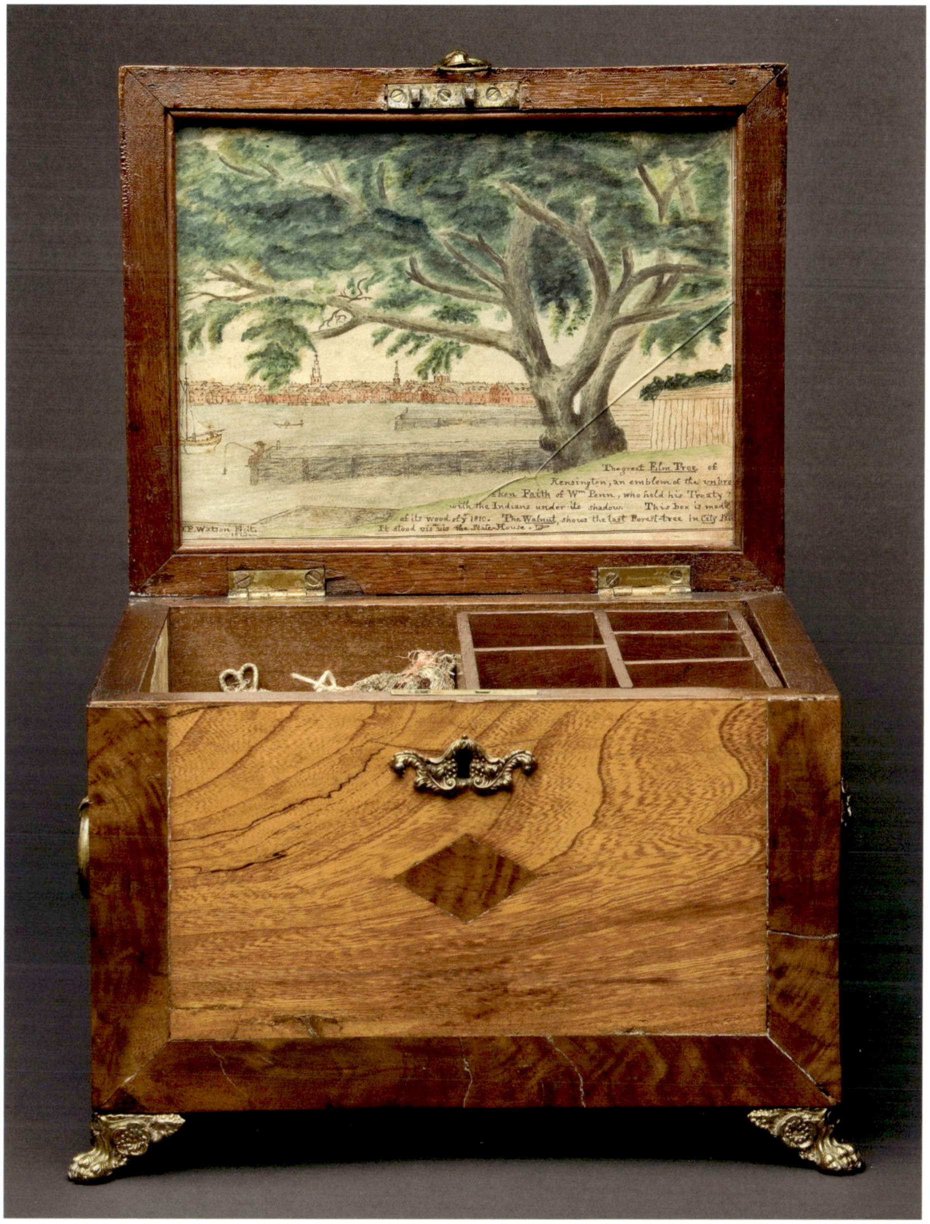

PLATE 20

John Fanning Watson (1779–1860)

Relic Box, 1810–1823

Elm, walnut, mahogany, brass, ink, watercolor on paper, 7¾ × 10¾ × 8½ inches. Museum purchase, courtesy of Winterthur Museum, Garden & Library

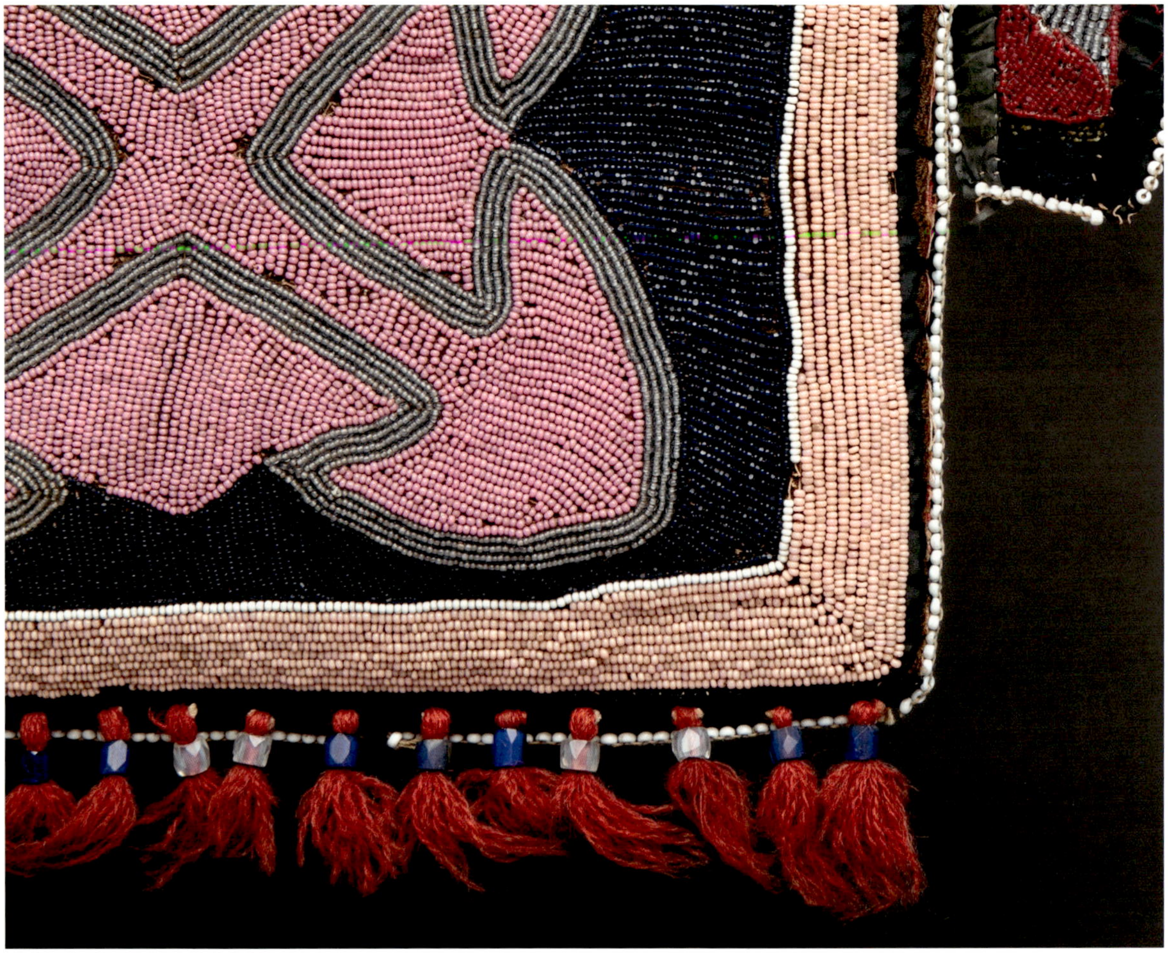

PLATE 21

Artist Unknown (Delaware)

Bandolier Bag, ca. 1850

Cotton wool, silk, and glass beads, 29 × 23 inches.
Photo by Addison Doty; courtesy of Thomas Cleary

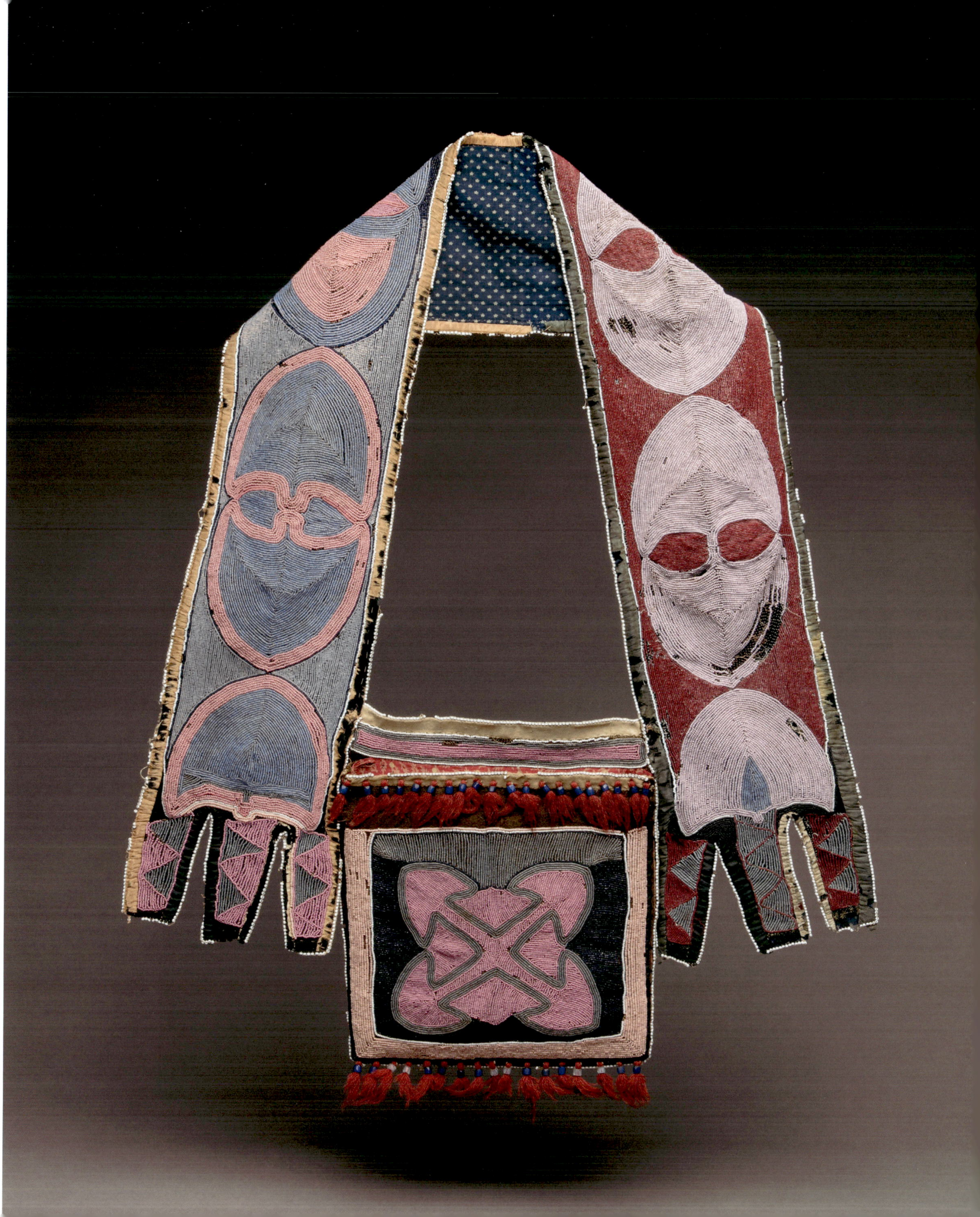

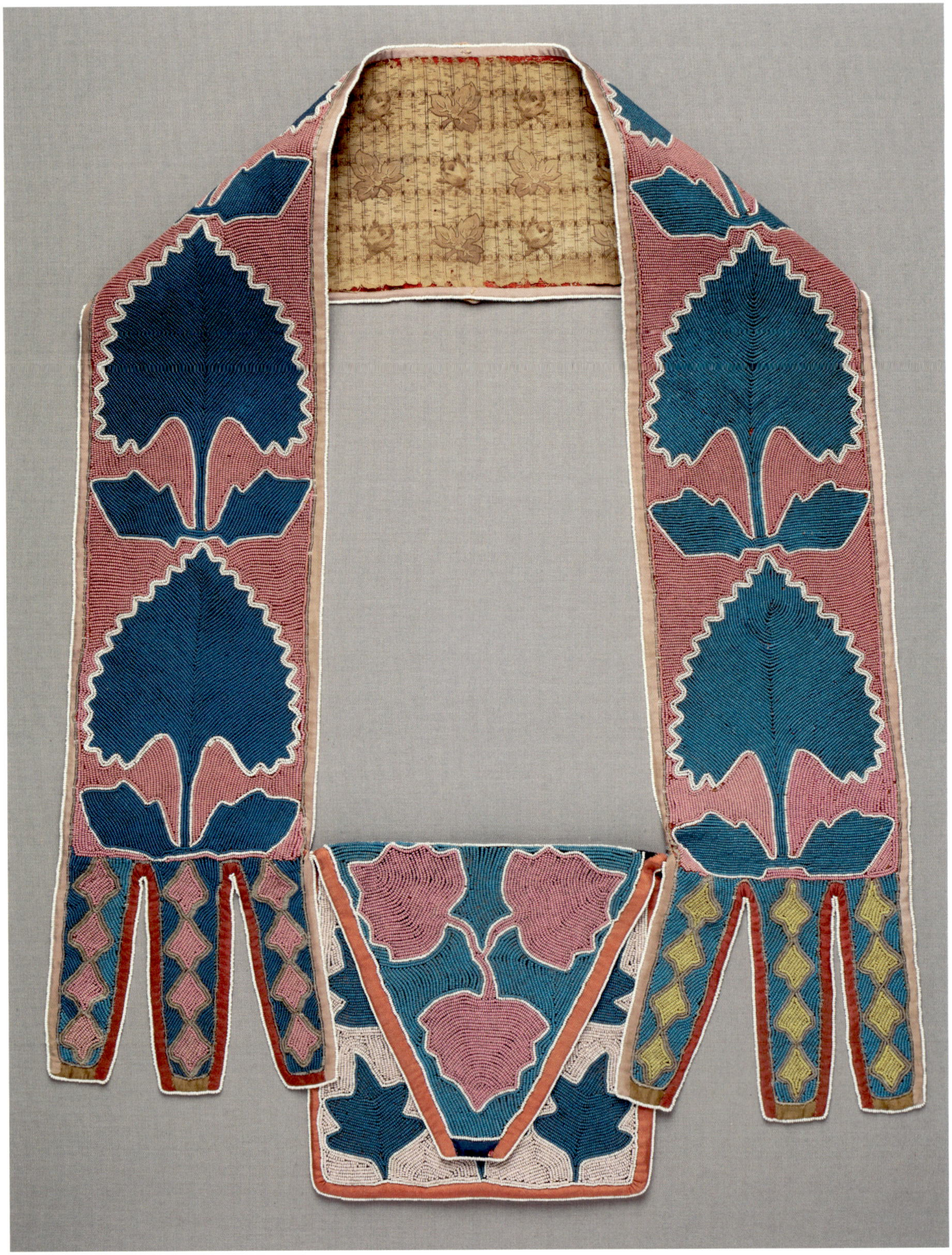

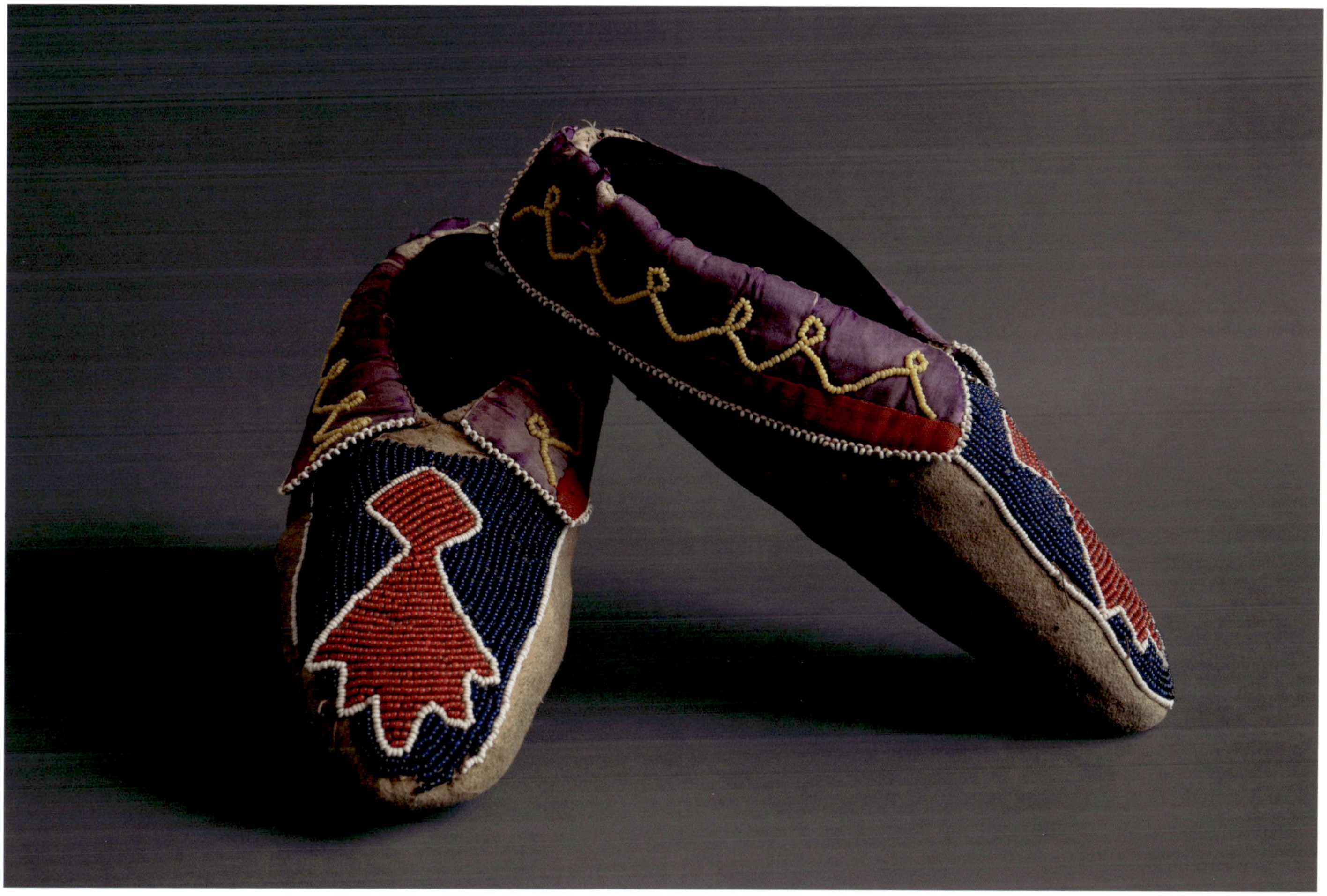

PLATE 22

Artist Unknown (Delaware)

Bandolier Bag, ca. 1850

Cotton, wool, silk, and glass beads, 28¼ × 21¼ × 2¼ inches. Brooklyn Museum, Frank L. Babbott Fund, 2021.41 (Photo: Brooklyn Museum)

PLATE 23

Artist Unknown (Delaware)

Moccasins, 19th century

Leather and glass beads, 9½ inches long. Photo by LeRoy Grafe; courtesy of Thomas Cleary

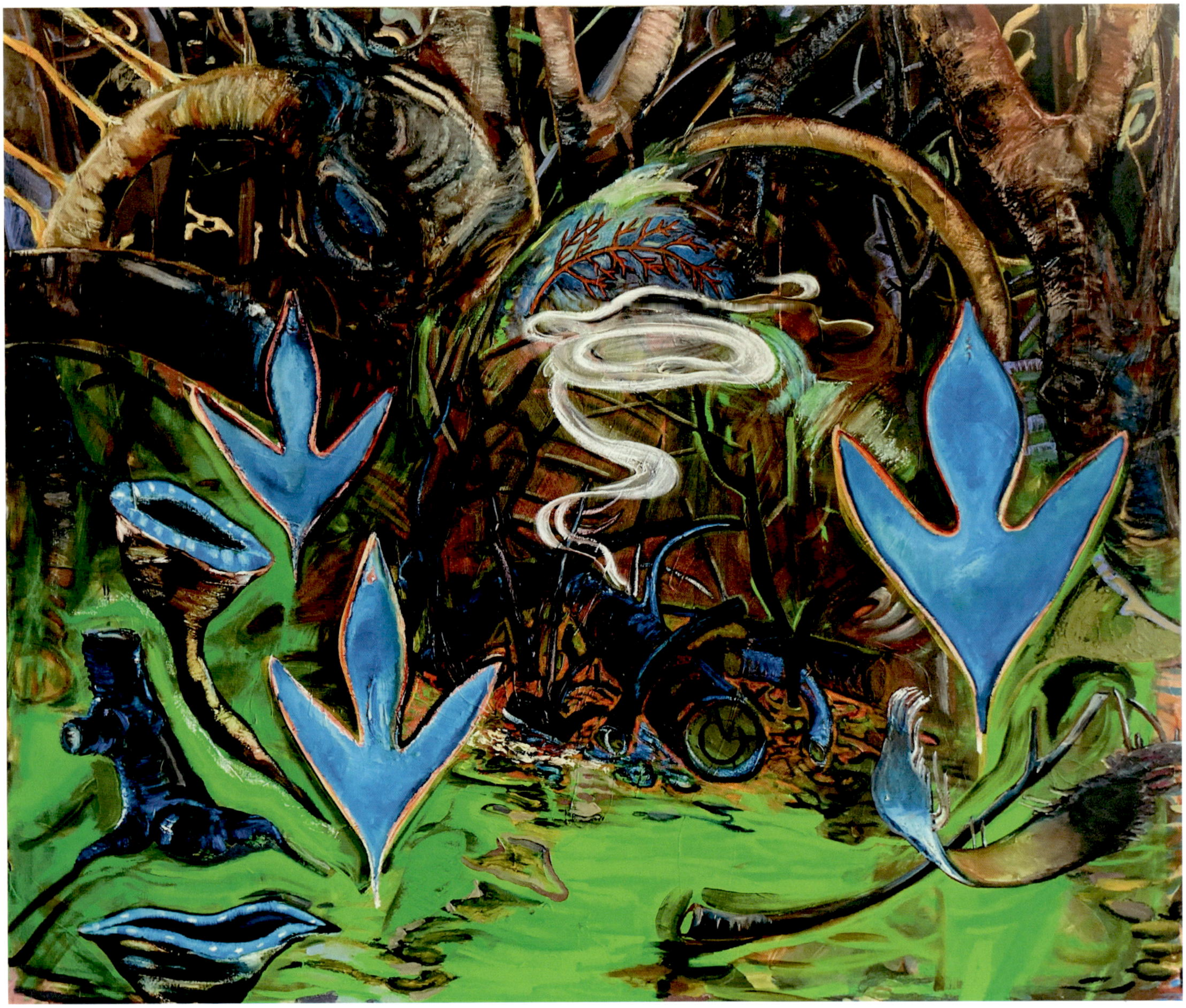

PLATE 24

Joe Baker (Delaware Tribe of Indians)

Three Sisters, 1997

Oil on canvas, 60 × 72 inches. The John and Susan Horseman Collection, courtesy of the Horseman Foundation

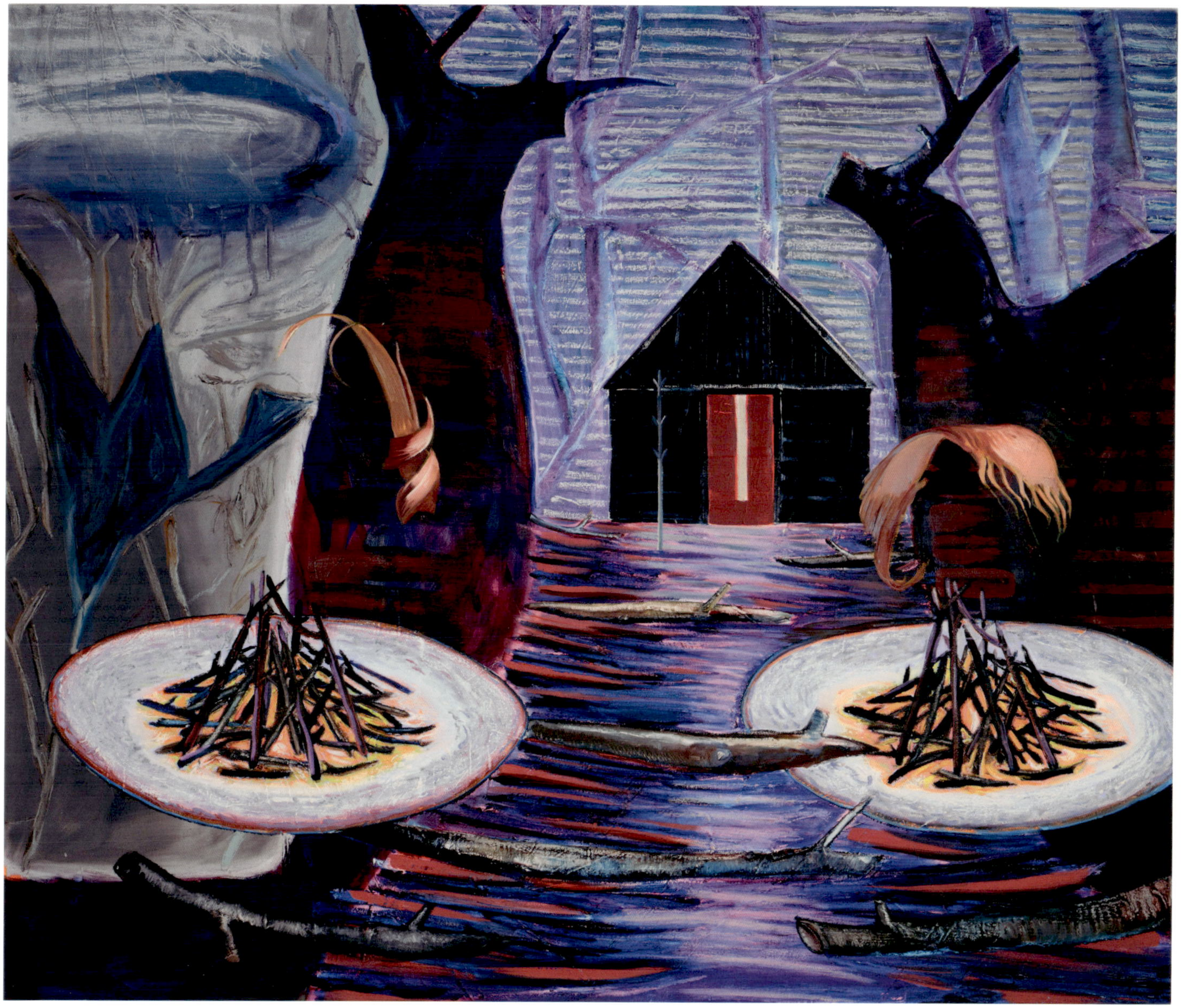

PLATE 25

Joe Baker (Delaware Tribe of Indians)

The Big House, 1997

Oil on canvas, 60 × 72 inches. Courtesy of the artist

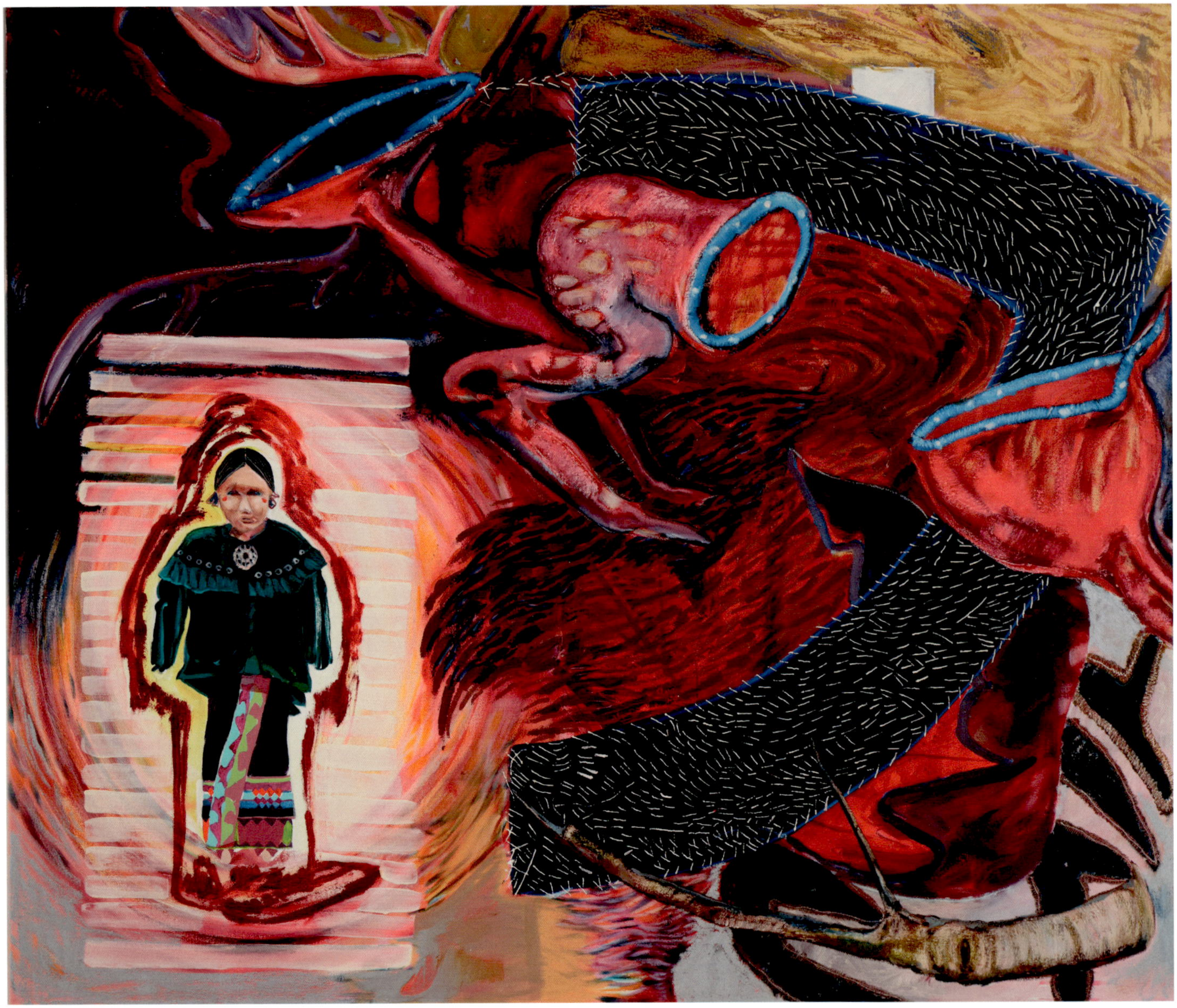

PLATE 26

Joe Baker (Delaware Tribe of Indians)

Doll Dance, 1997

Oil on canvas, 60 × 72 inches. Courtesy of the artist

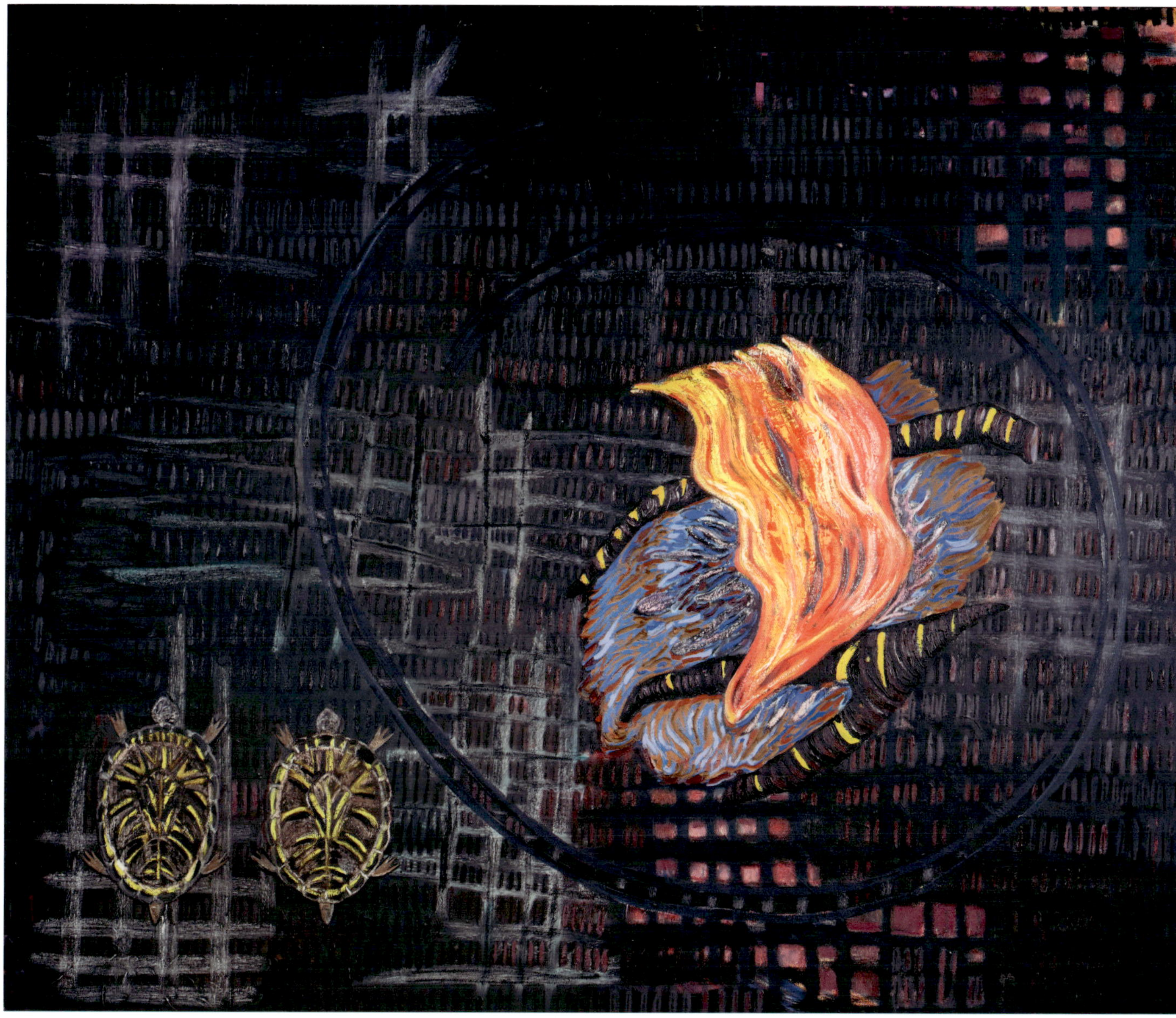

PLATE 27

Joe Baker (Delaware Tribe of Indians)

Stomp Dance, 1997

Oil on canvas, 66 × 78¼ inches. Courtesy of the artist

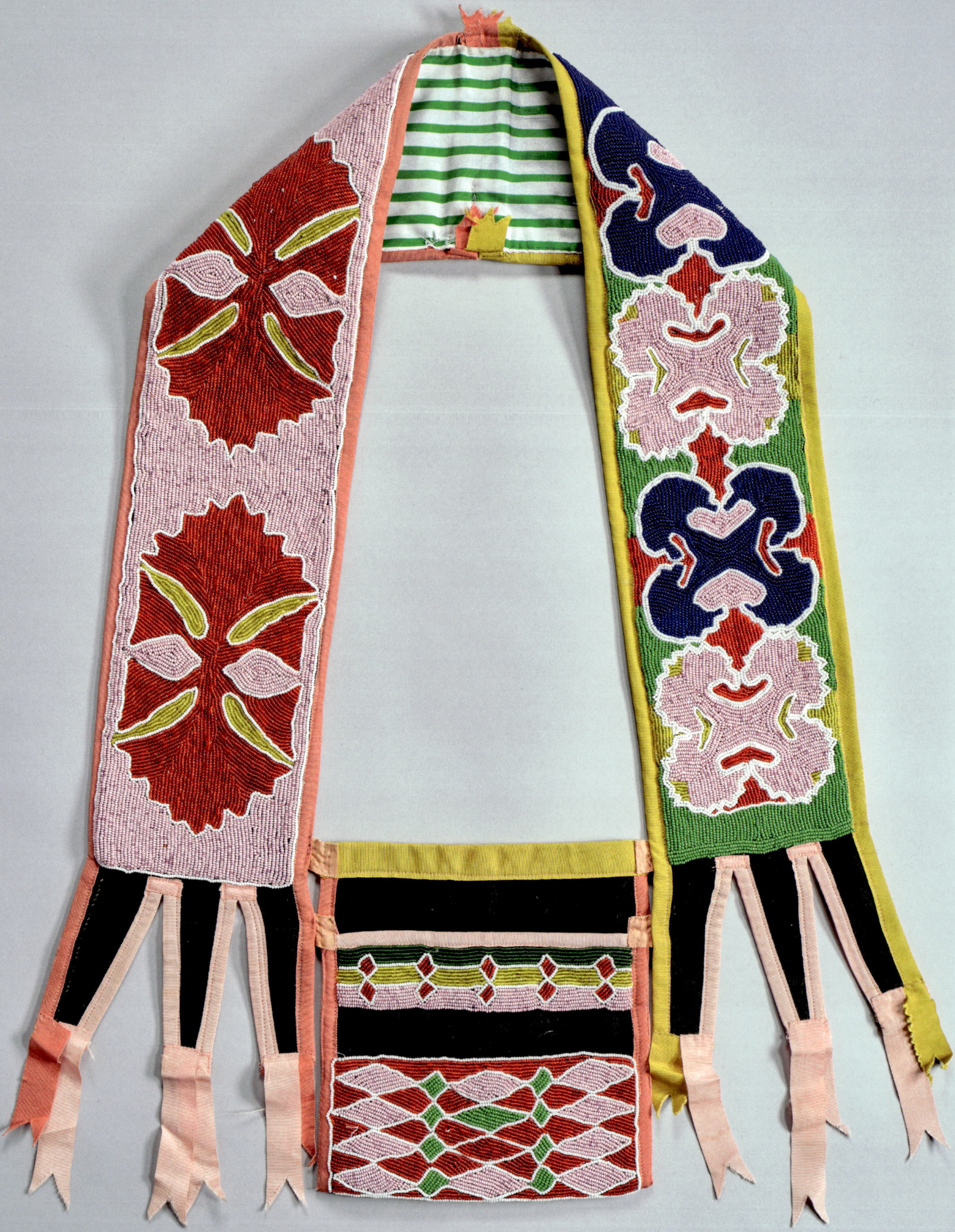

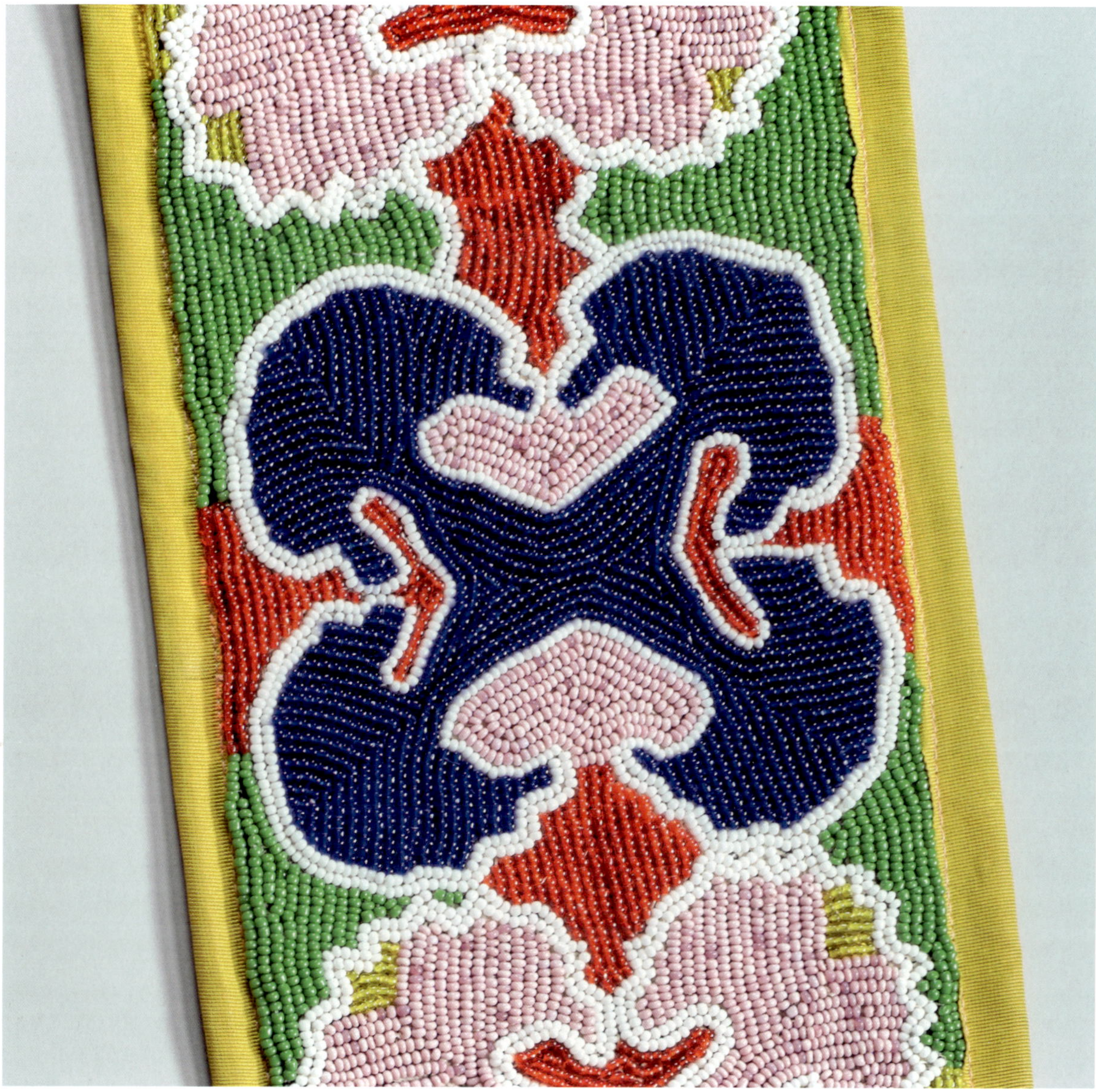

PLATE 28

Joe Baker (Delaware Tribe of Indians)

Bandolier Bag, 1999

Fabric, wool, and glass beads; strap: 31 × 6½ inches, bag: 9½ × 9 inches. Courtesy of the artist

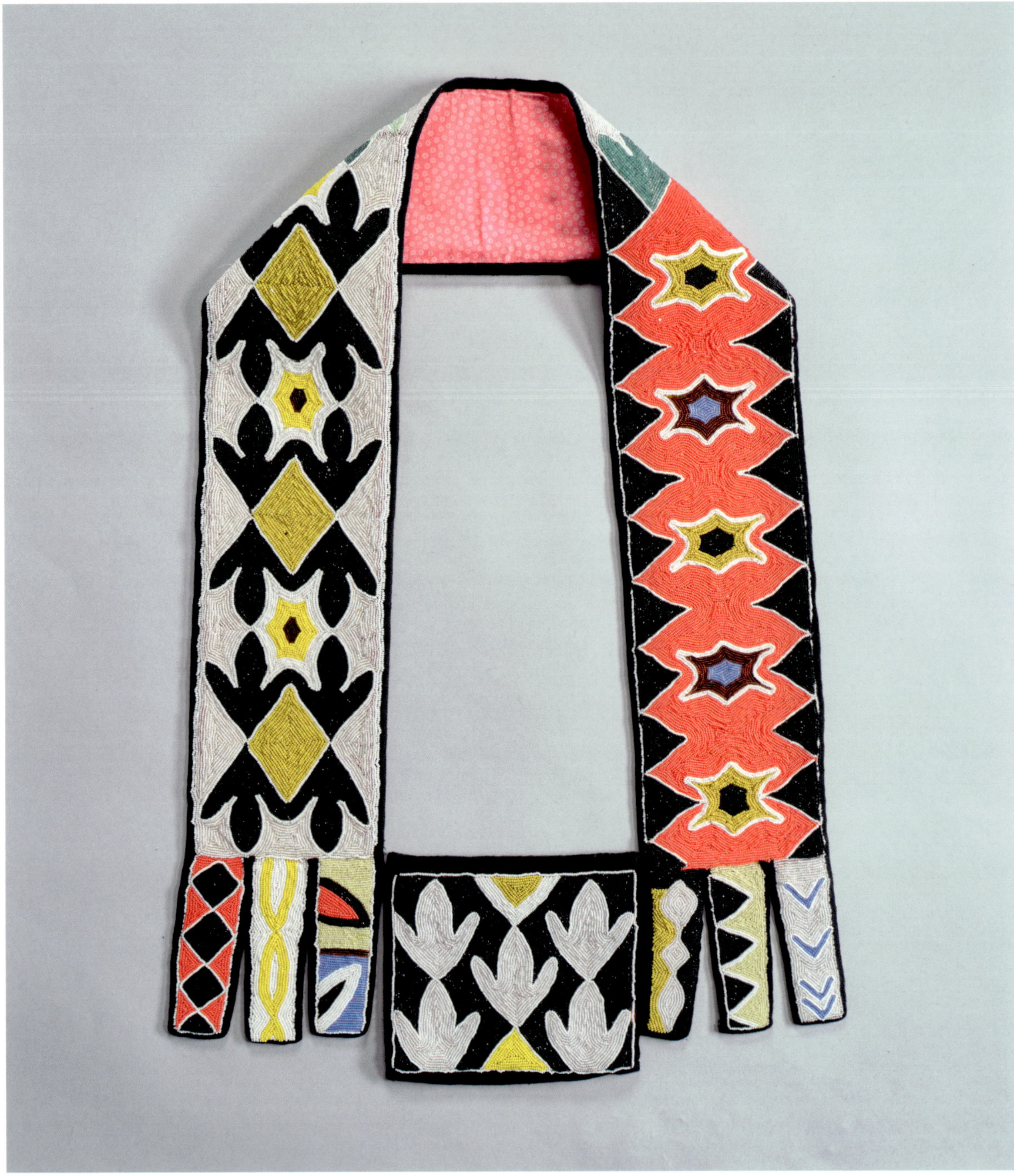

PLATE 29

Joe Baker (Delaware Tribe of Indians)

Bandolier Bag, 2014

Fabric, wool, and glass beads; strap: 24 × 7 inches, bag: 8¼ × 9 inches. Courtesy of the artist

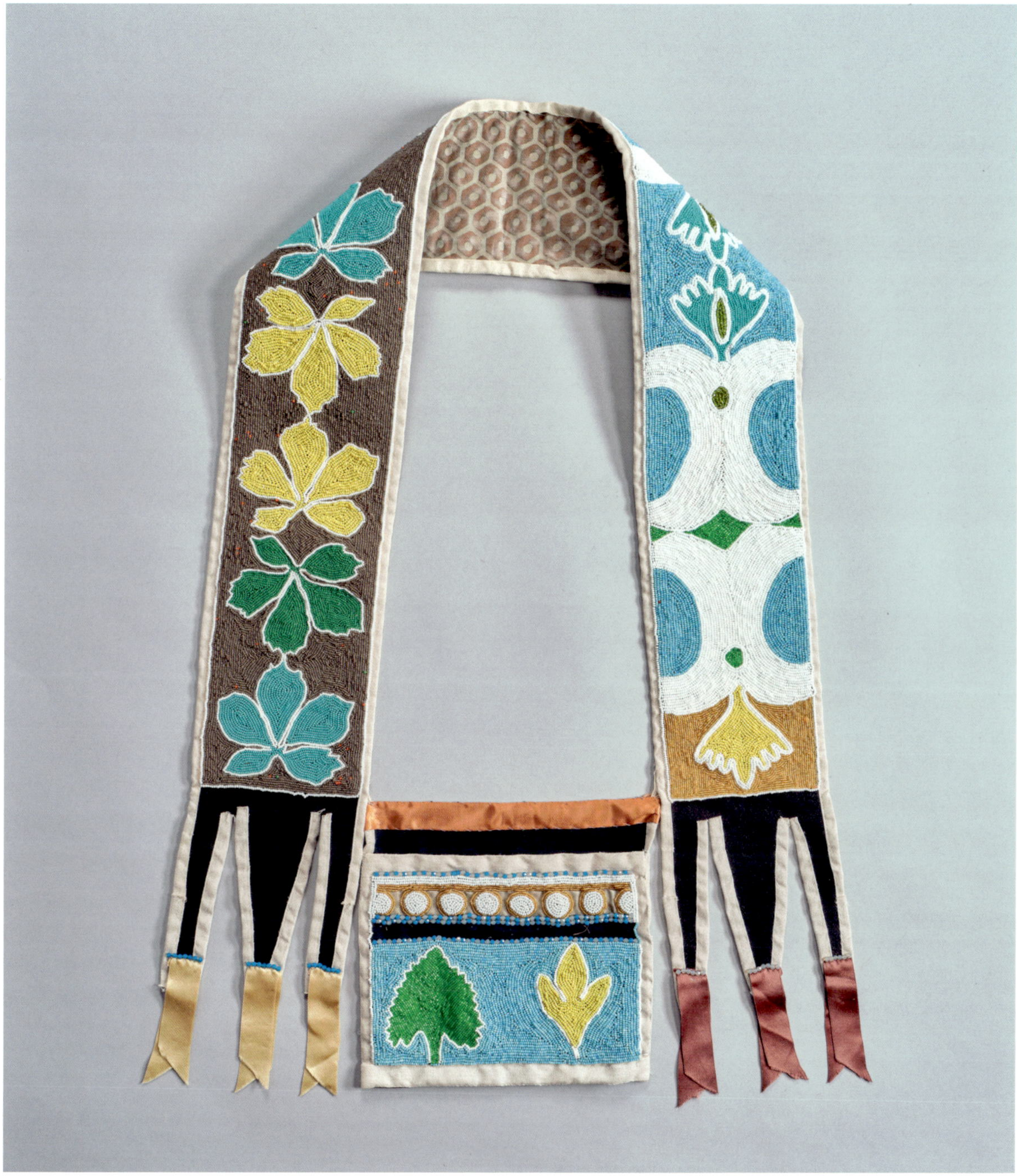

PLATE 30

Joe Baker (Delaware Tribe of Indians)

Bandolier Bag, 2021

Fabric, wool, and glass beads; strap: 30 × 5½ inches, bag: 9 × 9 inches. Courtesy of the artist

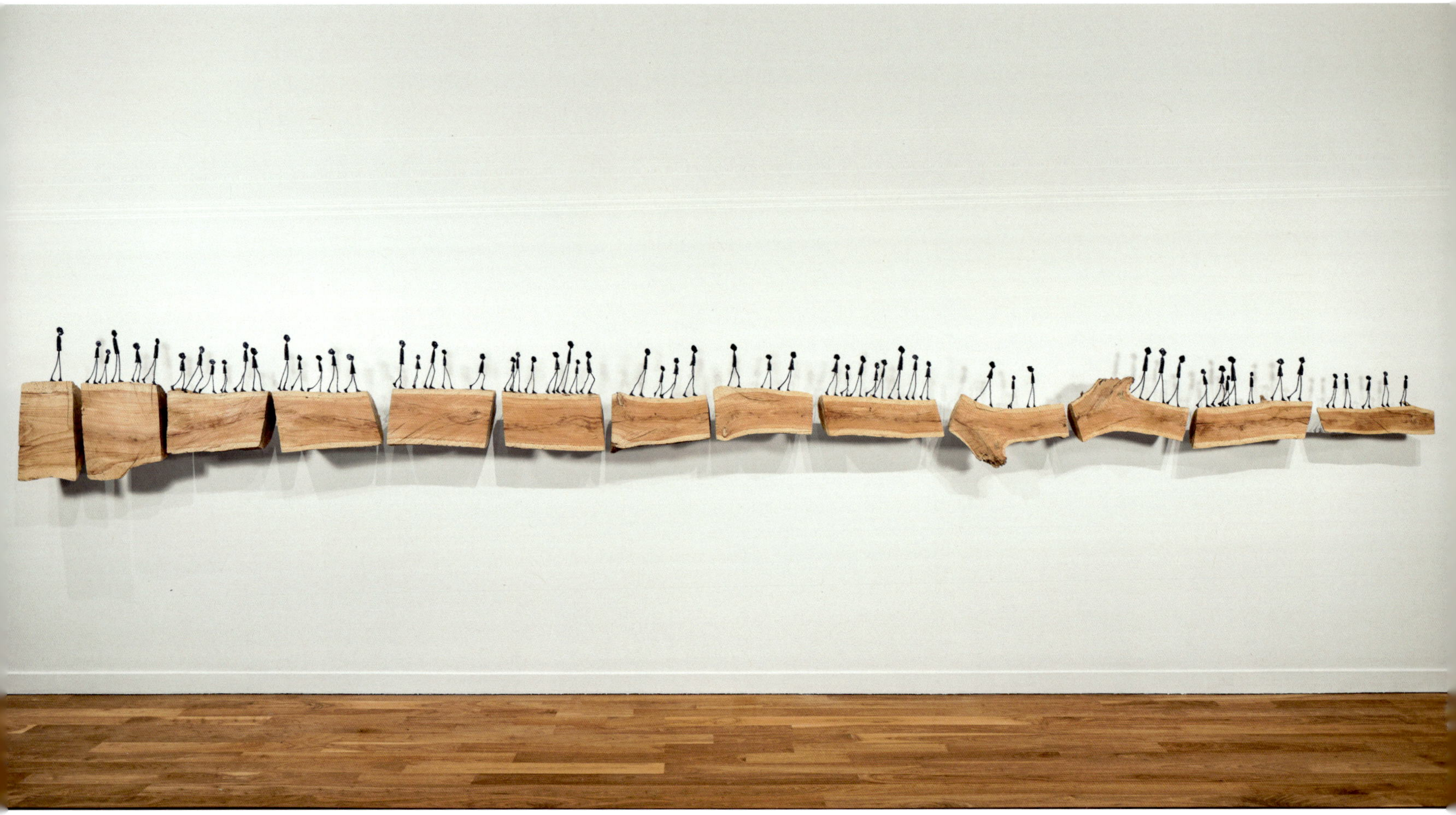

PLATE 31

Holly Wilson (Delaware Nation and Cherokee)

Bloodline, 2015

Bronze and locust wood, 29 inches × 22 feet × 9 inches. Courtesy of the artist

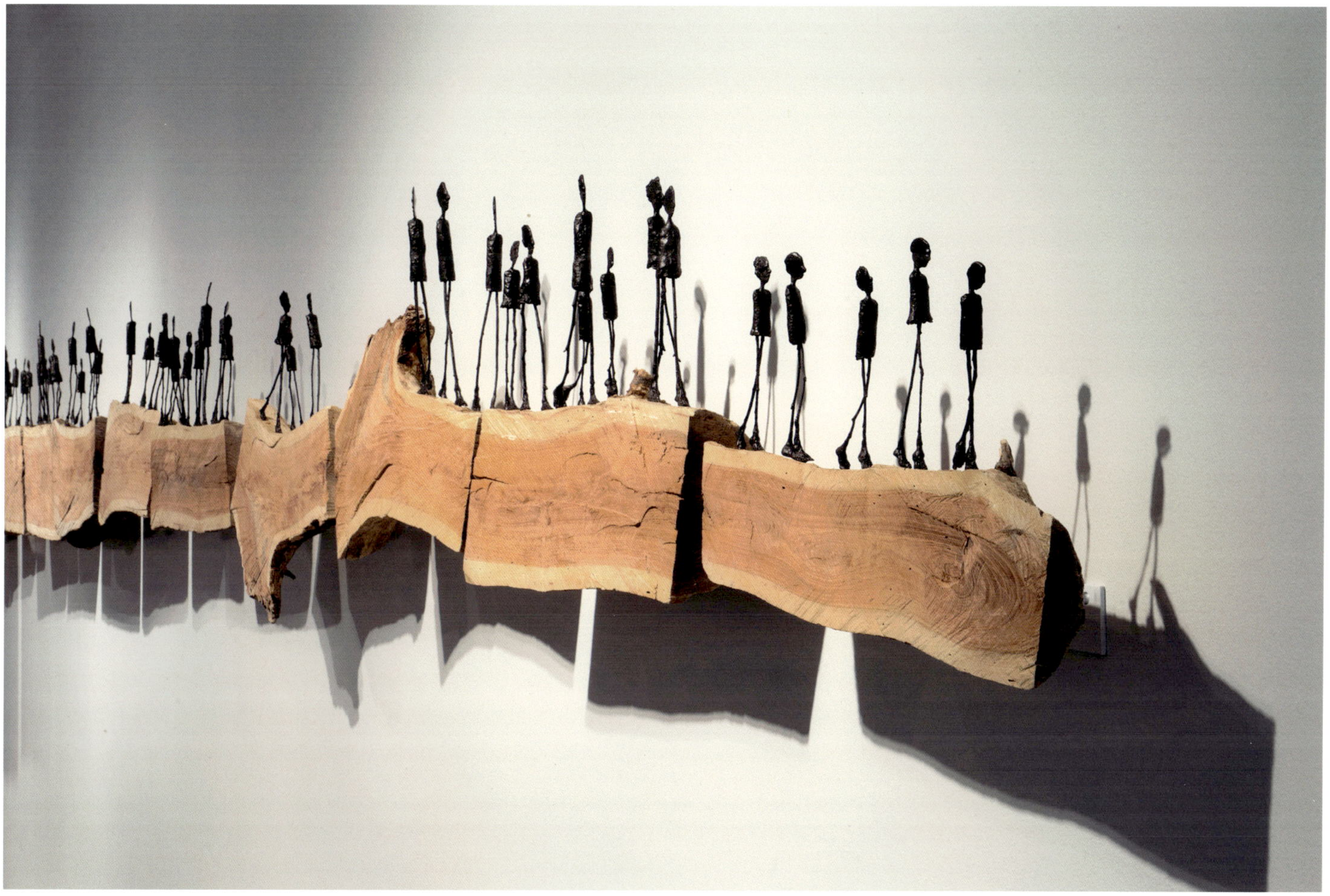

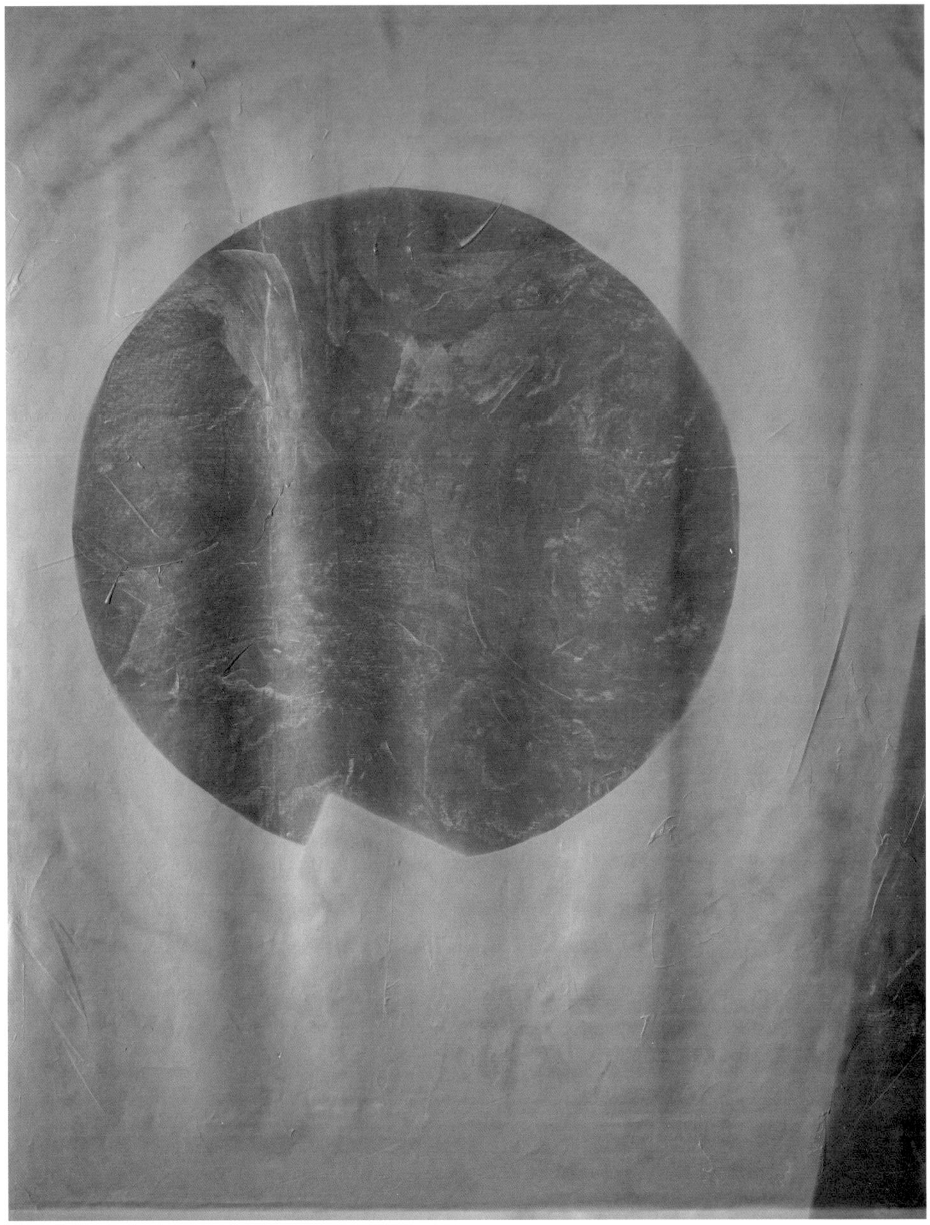

PLATE 32

Ahchipaptunhe (Delaware Tribe of Indians)

Hàki – Earth, Dirt, Ground or Soil, 2023

Acrylic on canvas, 63 × 88 inches. Courtesy of the artist

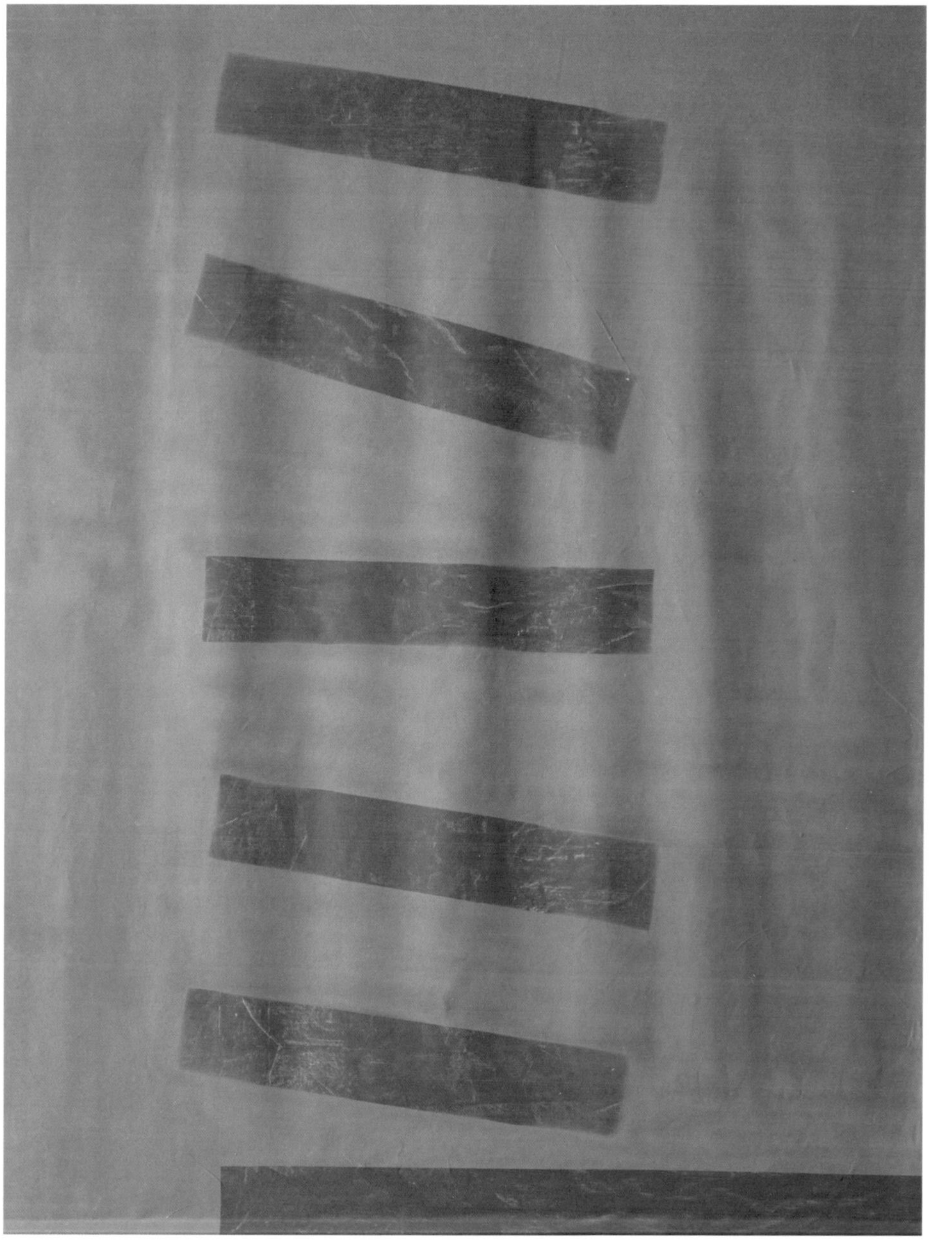

PLATE 33

Ahchipaptunhe (Delaware Tribe of Indians)

Niskëpèk – Dirty Water, 2023

Acrylic on canvas, 63 × 88 inches. Courtesy of the artist

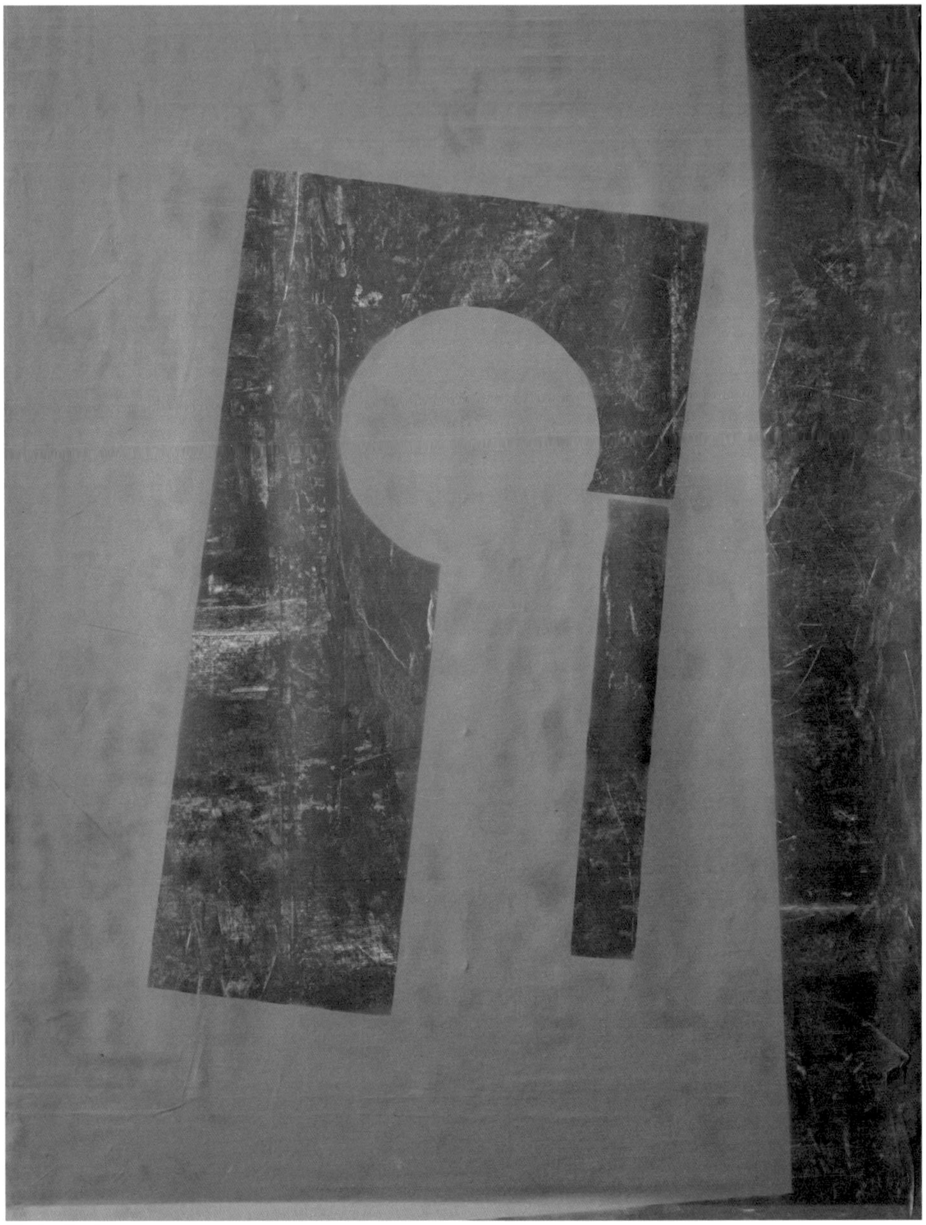

PLATE 34

Ahchipaptunhe (Delaware Tribe of Indians)

Lexeokàn – Breathing, 2023

Acrylic on canvas, 63 × 88 inches. Courtesy of the artist

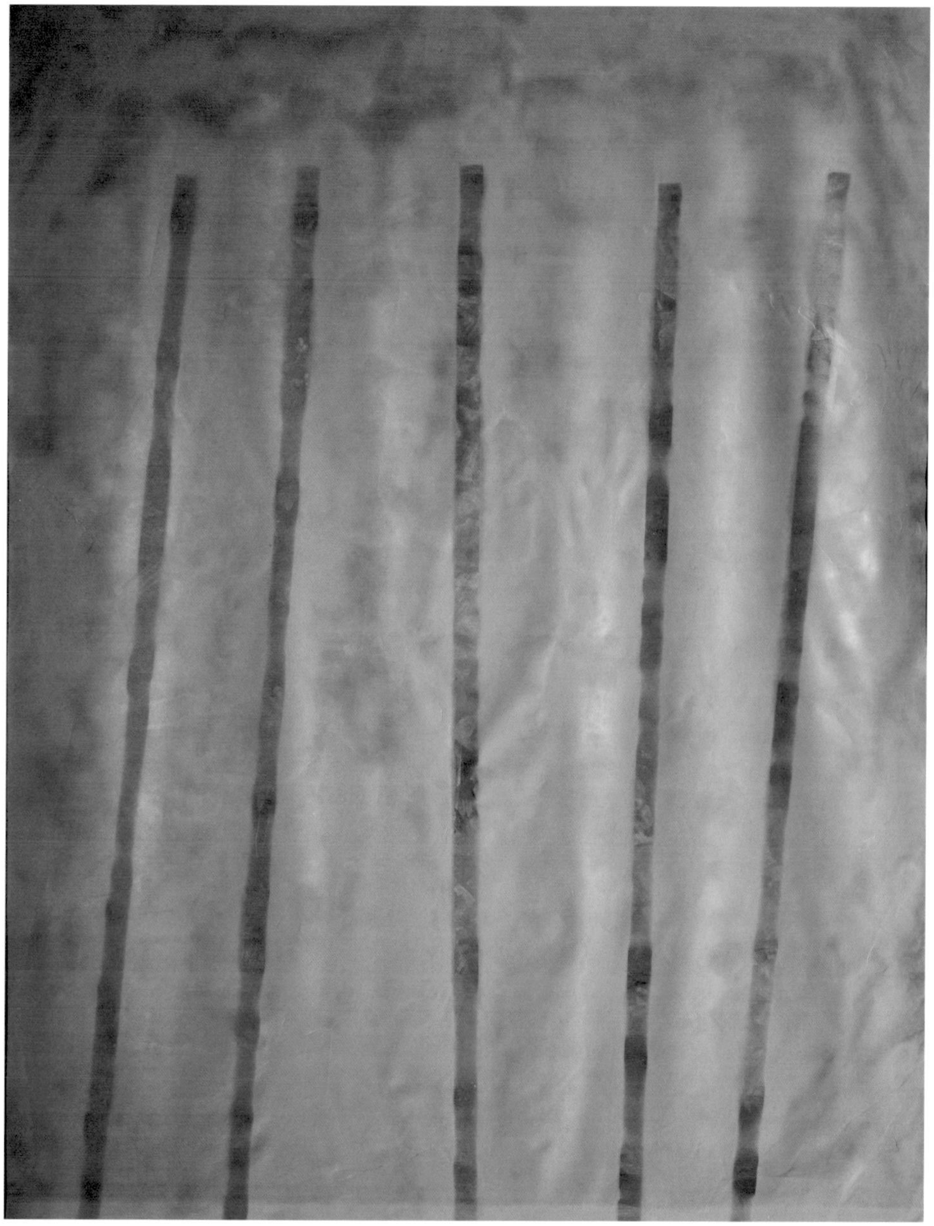

PLATE 35

Ahchipaptunhe (Delaware Tribe of Indians)

Tëntay – Fire, 2023

Acrylic on canvas, 63 × 88 inches. Courtesy of the artist

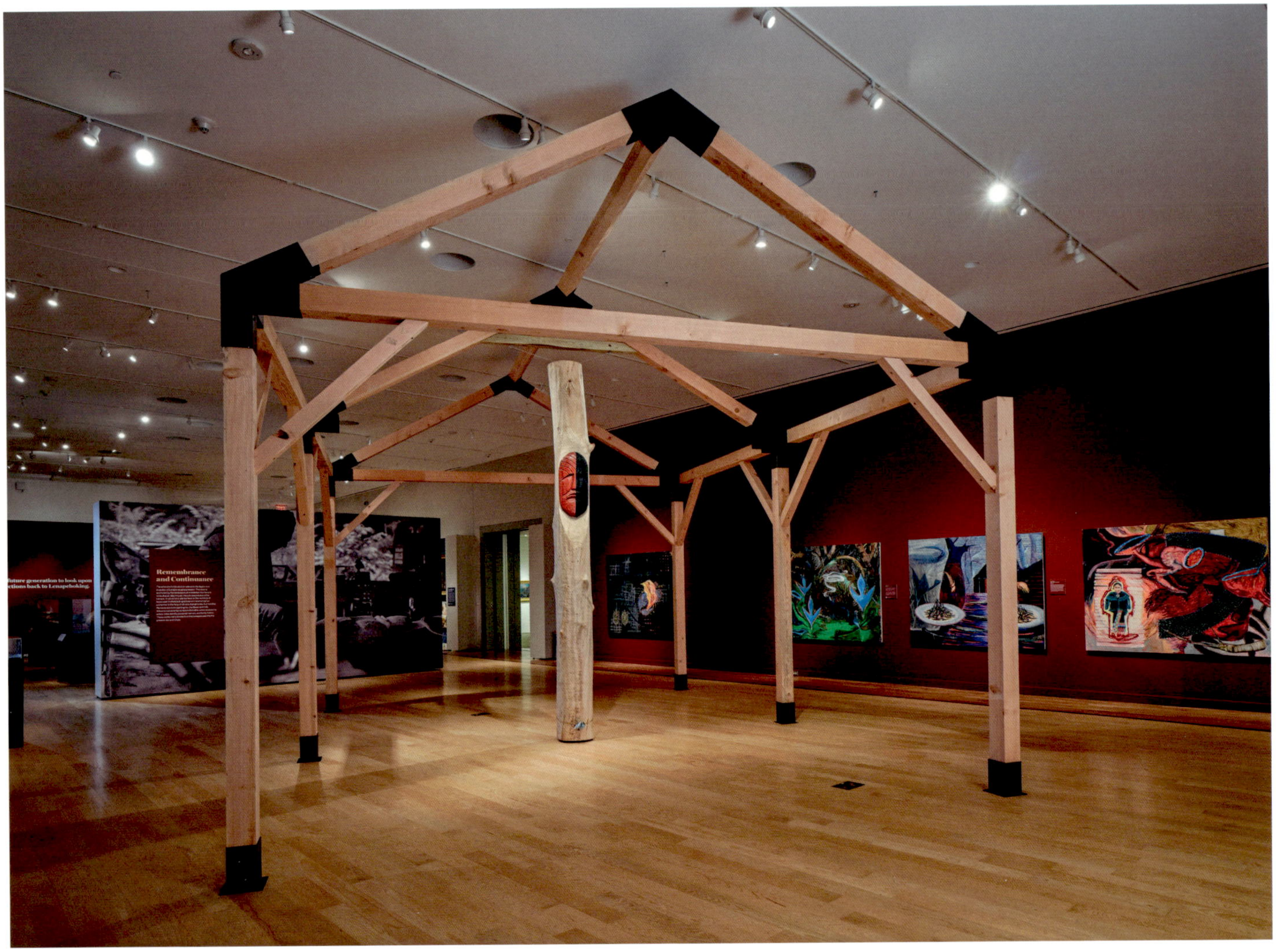

PLATE 36

Joe Baker (Delaware Tribe of Indians),
Michael Asbill, and student carvers

Remembrance, 2023

Big tooth aspen post and pine painted with charcoal and bloodroot in bear fat, 18 feet high × 13¾ inches diameter.
Courtesy of Lenape Center

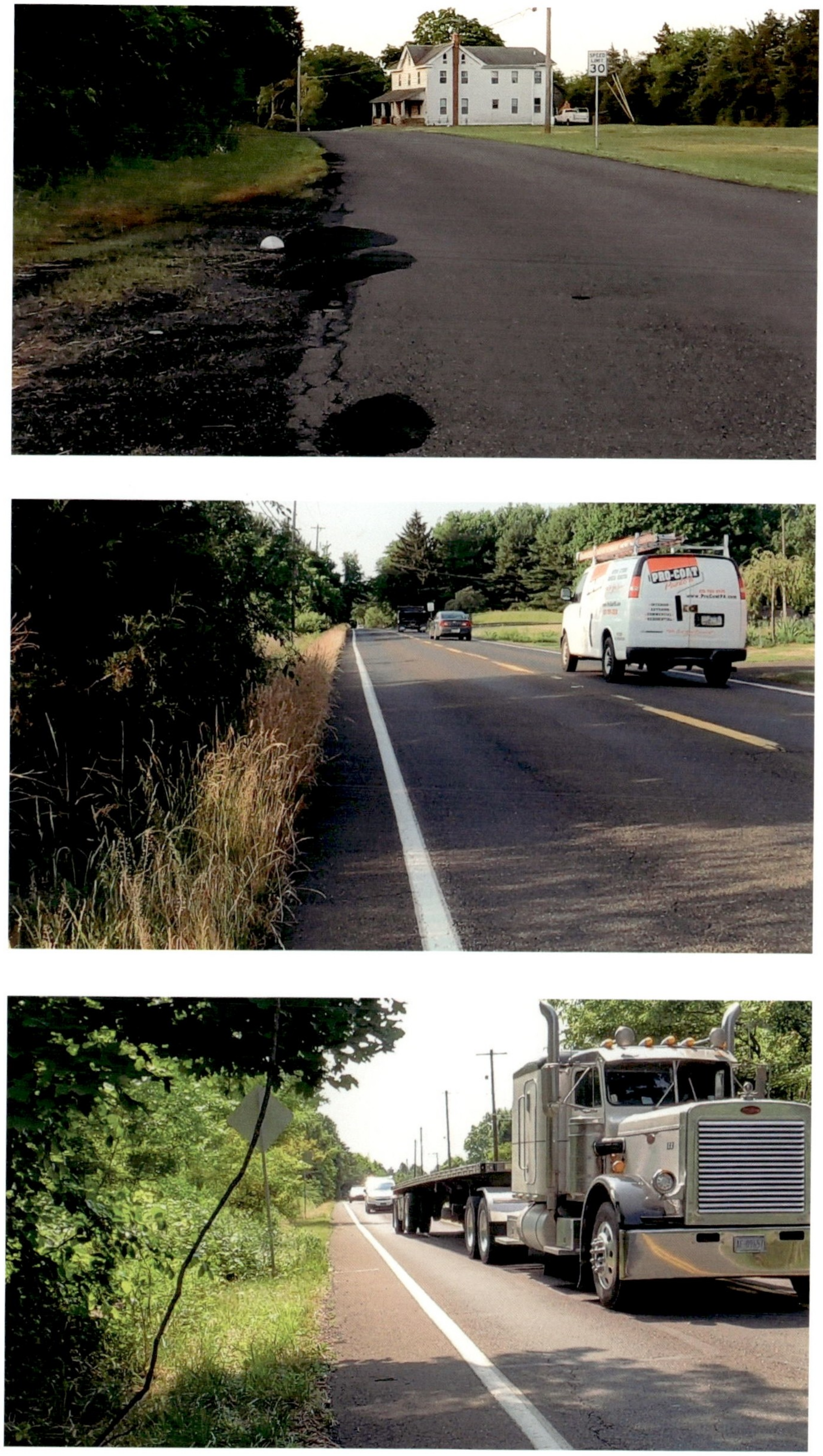

PLATE 37

Nathan Young (Delaware Tribe of Indians, Pawnee, and Kiowa)

Stills from *Alëmi pëmëske* (*He begins to walk*), 2023

Video and sound, 5 hours and 4 minutes. Courtesy of the artist

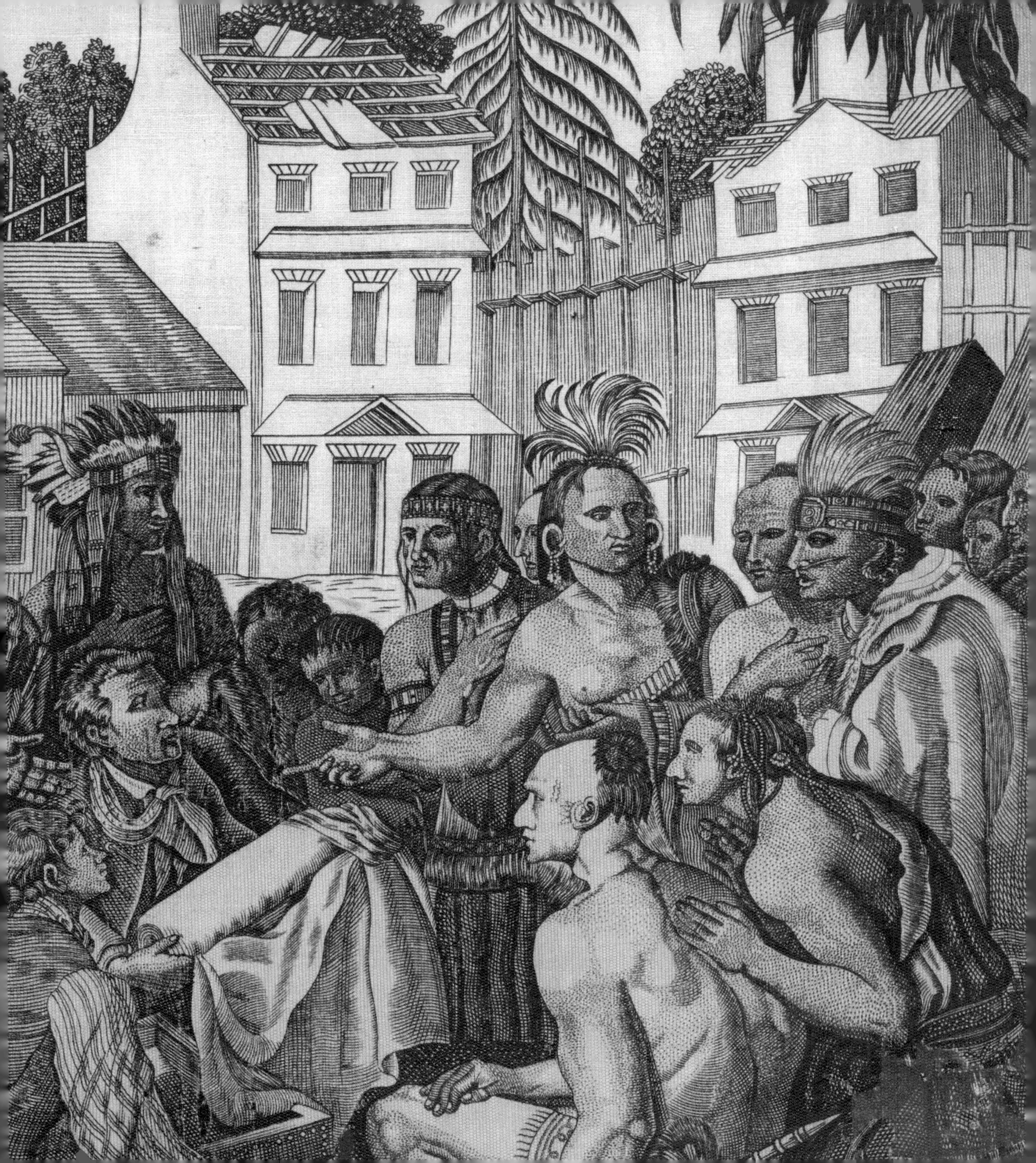

Contributors

JOE BAKER is an artist, educator, curator, and culture bearer who has been working in the field of Native arts for the past thirty years. He is an enrolled member of the Delaware Tribe of Indians of Oklahoma, adjunct professor at Columbia University's School of Social Work, and co-founder and executive director of Lenape Center in Manhattan. He serves as a board member for the Endangered Language Fund at CUNY, on the advisory committee for the National Public Art Consortium, New York, and as cultural advisor for the new CBS series *Ghosts*. Baker graduated from the University of Tulsa with a BFA degree in design and an MFA in painting and drawing, and he completed postgraduate study in the management development program at Harvard Graduate School of Education. His work is included in the permanent collection of the Metropolitan Museum of Art and numerous other museums and collections in the US and Canada, including the American Museum of Art and Design.

LAURA TURNER IGOE, PHD, is the Gerry and Marguerite Lenfest Chief Curator at the James A. Michener Art Museum in Doylestown, Pennsylvania. She previously held curatorial and research positions at the Philadelphia Museum of Art, Princeton University Art Museum, Harvard Art Museums, and the Barnes Foundation. She is the coeditor of *A Greene Country Towne: Philadelphia's Ecology in the Cultural Imagination*, and she has contributed essays to the journals *American Art*, *Panorama*, and *Commonplace*, and the exhibition catalogue *Nature's Nation: American Art and Environment*. At the Michener, she curated *Impressionism to Modernism: The Lenfest Collection of American Art* (2019), *Rising Tides: Contemporary Art and the Ecology of Water* (2020), and she co-curated *Through the Lens: Modern Photography in the Delaware Valley* (2021) and *Daring Design: The Impact of Three Women on Wharton Esherick's Craft* (2021–2022).

JOEL WHITNEY is the author of *Finks: How the CIA Tricked the World's Best Writers*. With Joe Baker and Hadrien Coumans, he is a co-editor of *Lenapehoking: An Anthology* and a founder and former editor of *Guernica: A Magazine of Global Arts & Politics*. His writing appears or is forthcoming in the *New York Times*, *The Believer*, *The Baffler*, *Newsweek*, *Boston Review*, *Salon*, *NPR*, *The New Republic*, and *Jacobin*. His collection of linked essays, *Flights: Progressives on the Run*, will appear in early 2024.

Detail of plate 10

This book is published in conjunction with the exhibition *Never Broken: Visualizing Lenape Histories*, presented at the James A. Michener Art Museum, Doylestown, Pennsylvania, from September 9, 2023, to January 14, 2024.

Never Broken: Visualizing Lenape Histories is one in a series of American art exhibitions created through a multi-year, multi-institutional partnership formed by the Philadelphia Museum of Art as part of the Art Bridges Cohort Program.

Art Bridges + Philadelphia Museum of Art

This exhibition and catalogue were supported by a generous grant from the Henry Luce Foundation.

HENRY LUCE FOUNDATION

Additional support was provided by Michener Art Museum's Corporate Business Partners, Eiseman Construction, Inc., and the Dolfinger-McMahon Foundation.

This catalogue is presented in collaboration with Lenape Center.

LENAPE CENTER

Library of Congress Control Number: 2023945897
ISBN 978-1-879636-16-3

Published by the James A. Michener Art Museum
www.michenerartmuseum.org

Distributed by the University of Pennsylvania Press
www.pennpress.org

Produced by Marquand Books, Seattle
www.marquandbooks.com

Edited by Bruno George
Designed by Thomas Eykemans
Typeset in Miller by Brynn Warriner
Proofread by Ted Gilley
Color management by I/O Color, Seattle
Printed and bound by Brilliant Graphics

Jacket: Detail of plate 22
Jacket flaps: Detail of plate 8
Pages 2–3: Detail of plate 31
Pages 52–53: Detail of plate 10

Photography Credits:

Pages 12–13, 26–27, and 39–41: *Never Broken: Visualizing Lenape Histories*, exhibition installation, James A. Michener Art Museum, 2023. Photos by Christian Giannelli

Plates 1–7 and 25–36: Photos by Christian Giannelli